Tulsa King Unveiled

Tulsa King Unveiled

Matthew Petchinsky

Tulsa King Unveiled: A Thrilling Guide to Stallone's Mafia Masterpiece

By: Matthew Petchinsky

Disclaimer for "Tulsa King Unveiled: A Thrilling Guide to Stallone's Mafia Masterpiece"

The contents of this book, *Tulsa King Unveiled: A Thrilling Guide to Stallone's Mafia Masterpiece*, are intended for entertainment, discussion, and educational purposes only. This book is an opinion piece and a work of fan expression; it is not a definitive source or an official account of the events, characters, or portrayals in *Tulsa King*. It does not reflect any official position, endorsement, or approval by Sylvester Stallone, the creators, producers, or distributors of the *Tulsa King* series. The opinions expressed within these pages are solely those of the author and do not represent facts, the intent of the show's creators, or the exact motivations behind any storyline, character arc, or decision made in the show.

Additionally, all references to scenes, characters, or events from *Tulsa King* are based on the author's personal interpretations, impressions, and analyses. Readers should not assume that any perspectives, interpretations, or extrapolations made in this book accurately reflect the creators' views, intentions, or factual representations. This book has been crafted by a fan for the enjoyment of other fans, and as such, is neither exhaustive nor an authoritative source on *Tulsa King* or any individuals involved in its production.

The author encourages readers to view this guide as an exploration of themes, characters, and storylines rather than as factual commentary. Fans are invited to draw their conclusions and interpretations and to enjoy the show independently of the perspectives offered here. No copyright infringement or endorsement is implied; all rights to *Tulsa King* and its related intellectual properties remain with their rightful owners.

Introduction to *Tulsa King Unveiled: A Thrilling Guide to Stallone's Mafia Masterpiece*

What is *Tulsa King*?

Tulsa King is a captivating crime drama series that follows the journey of Dwight "The General" Manfredi, a high-ranking New York mafia capo portrayed by Sylvester Stallone. After spending a grueling 25 years in prison for his loyalty to his criminal family, Dwight emerges with a mixture of grit, wisdom, and pent-up ambition. However, his return to freedom takes an unexpected twist: instead of reclaiming his place in New York, he's exiled to Tulsa, Oklahoma—a place as foreign to him as his newly adopted smartphone. Tasked by his mafia family with establishing a new empire in this unexpected terrain, Dwight must adapt to a world that's moved on without him.

Set in a dusty, rough-edged Tulsa, far from the bustling streets of New York, the show paints a compelling picture of one man's determination to wield power and control in an environment that's more alien than familiar. Dwight's mission is a blend of adaptation, calculation, and resilience, as he seeks to build a criminal network from scratch while navigating a landscape that's technologically, socially, and culturally miles apart from the world he once knew.

Through a fascinating interplay of action, drama, and humor, *Tulsa King* explores themes of loyalty, adaptation, and the pursuit of redemption amid morally gray choices. It's a story that delves into the essence of survival, both in the criminal underworld and within a man who has lost everything except his unyielding will to rise again.

Why You Should Watch *Tulsa King*

For fans of action, crime dramas, and character-driven storytelling, *Tulsa King* offers a fresh, engaging experience that combines the best of these genres, headlined by a remarkable performance from Stallone himself.

1. Stallone's Stellar Performance

Sylvester Stallone, known for his unforgettable roles in action films like *Demolition Man* and *Judge Dredd*, brings a magnetic presence to *Tulsa King* as Dwight Manfredi. Stallone's portrayal of Dwight is a masterclass in blending toughness with nuanced emotion. He dominates the screen with a blend of power and charisma, commanding each scene with his classic "tough guy" demeanor while imbuing Dwight with layers of vulnerability, humor, and depth. Stallone's seasoned experience and intensity elevate the character from a traditional mafia archetype to a memorable antihero who viewers can't help but root for—even as he walks a morally ambiguous path.

2. A Unique Combination of Crime Drama, Action, and Humor

What truly sets *Tulsa King* apart is its unique mix of crime, action, and humor, an approach that stands out in today's TV landscape. The show's foundation in mafia crime drama is enriched with bursts of explosive action sequences that showcase Dwight's ruthlessness and street smarts. Yet it's the unexpected moments of levity, often arising from Dwight's attempts to navigate his new world, that make the show even more compelling. His interactions with the locals of Tulsa, from reluctant allies to suspicious rivals, often lead to humor that lightens the show's darker undertones and reveals the character's human side. This balance between intense action and well-placed humor makes *Tulsa King* an exhilarating yet grounded watch.

3. A Gritty, Yet Compelling, Exploration of the Underworld

While *Tulsa King* shares some thematic roots with classic mafia narratives, it presents a fresh take on underworld storytelling by shifting the stage to a seemingly quiet Oklahoma town. Tulsa serves as an unlikely yet fitting backdrop, amplifying the challenges Dwight faces and emphasizing the grit and determination required to establish his influence in unfamiliar territory. The show's gritty storytelling style is tempered with moments that make it accessible and relatable, allowing viewers to be drawn into Dwight's world and root for him despite his morally ambiguous motives. With Stallone at the helm, *Tulsa King* delves into the human side of crime and power, making it one of the most captivating shows available today.

In *Tulsa King*, you'll find a thrilling and thoughtful series that captures Stallone's trademark intensity and charisma, backed by an ensemble cast, a unique setting, and a storyline that draws viewers into a complex world of crime, loyalty, and redemption. Whether you're a fan of classic mob stories, intense character dramas, or Stallone's cinematic legacy, *Tulsa King* offers something fresh and engaging—an experience worth watching, dissecting, and discussing in depth.

Chapter 1: Introduction to Dwight "The General" Manfredi
A Man of Loyalty, Discipline, and Iron Will

Dwight "The General" Manfredi, portrayed by the legendary Sylvester Stallone, stands as a figure of deep loyalty, personal code, and resilience. As a high-ranking capo in a New York mafia family, Dwight earned his reputation as a man of unbreakable loyalty and unwavering discipline—qualities that came at a high cost. He sacrificed 25 years of his life behind bars, choosing silence over betrayal. This silence wasn't just about the law or a show of defiance; it was an act of loyalty and self-preservation, embodying the complex and often harsh code of conduct in the mafia world. This level of commitment is rare, even among hardened criminals, marking Dwight as someone who commands respect and admiration, both in the underworld and from audiences.

Dwight's mafia nickname, "The General," speaks volumes about his role and character. He's more than a hitman or an enforcer; he's a strategist, a leader, and someone who not only wields power but also has a deep understanding of it. Throughout his time in the mob, Dwight demonstrated a talent for orchestrating large operations, making critical decisions under pressure, and managing people with an iron grip. As a general of sorts, he embodies both the protective and ruthless elements associated with such a title, often placing the welfare of the "family" above his own needs and desires. Dwight's commitment to this code is what makes his journey after prison both poignant and fraught with complexity.

Life Before Prison: Building a Legacy

Before his incarceration, Dwight Manfredi was a force in the New York underworld, a figure known for both his ruthlessness and his calculated approach. Unlike some mafiosi who operate solely through brute force, Dwight was respected for his strategic mind. In a world where violence and intimidation were necessary tools, Dwight wielded them with purpose, using fear and respect interchangeably to maintain his status. He was known to make critical decisions, often balancing loyalty with self-preservation, and his reputation as a problem-solver and a "fixer" made him indispensable to his mafia family.

Dwight's early years are shrouded in a sense of mystery, though it's clear he came up through the ranks in classic mob fashion, likely proving himself in smaller roles before ascending to more influential positions. His reputation wasn't built on simple violence but on a calculated approach to power. The weight of his name alone was enough to elicit fear and respect within his family's circles, setting him apart as a figure who wasn't just a soldier but a commander. He earned his title as "The General" long before his imprisonment, a title that carried with it a sense of both pride and isolation—a heavy burden for a man bound to the mob's moral ambiguity.

25 Years Behind Bars: The Price of Loyalty

Dwight's decision to endure 25 years in prison speaks volumes about his loyalty, resilience, and personal code. He remained silent, refusing to give up his comrades or cooperate with law enforcement, an act that demanded unimaginable inner strength. During his time in prison, Dwight witnessed the world evolve rapidly outside his cell walls—technological advancements, cultural shifts, and even the mafia's role in society changed. He knew, however, that his loyalty would come at a cost, yet he was willing to bear it, driven by a deep sense of honor to his family.

In prison, Dwight became a quiet leader, likely earning respect from fellow inmates and guards alike. While this isn't shown explicitly, it's clear that Dwight's willpower and presence influenced those around him. He emerged with a sense of discipline and wisdom, a man who had not only survived but adapted to his environment. For Dwight, prison wasn't just a period of waiting but a test of endurance and character. Every day served reinforced his identity as "The General," a man who was both respected and feared, even within the prison walls.

Released, but Displaced: Exiled to Tulsa

Upon his release, Dwight expected to return to New York, perhaps with the hope of reclaiming his place in the mafia or even settling into a quieter life after serving his family so loyally. Instead, he finds himself exiled to Tulsa, Oklahoma—a drastic and disorienting relocation far from his familiar world. This is no gentle retirement; it's an exile, a subtle rejection of his value and influence. For Dwight, this new journey becomes an unexpected mission to rebuild himself from the ground up in an unfamiliar land with no allies, no resources, and no established power.

In Tulsa, Dwight is faced with the complexities of reintegration, a task that's challenging even without the added burden of criminal ambition. He has to not only readjust to the world outside prison but also figure out how to build a new empire from scratch in a city that operates by a different set of rules. The absence of the familiar New York power structures and networks forces him to rely on his instincts and resourcefulness. In this barren, uncharted territory, Dwight is like a general without an army—determined to establish his power base, rebuild his legacy, and prove his relevance in a world that has largely moved on without him.

Adapting to Modern Realities

Perhaps one of the most compelling aspects of Dwight's journey is watching him navigate the modern world—a world filled with smartphones, social media, and surveillance technology. These changes represent a constant challenge for Dwight, who must adapt to the present without abandoning the old-school tactics and values that define him. His interactions with modern technology, often marked by a blend of humor and frustration, highlight the generational and cultural gap between Dwight and the world he's now operating in.

While the technological landscape may be new, Dwight's skills as a strategist, leader, and survivor are as relevant as ever. He brings his experience, intuition, and calculated ruthlessness to Tulsa, utilizing his understanding of human behavior to recruit new allies and intimidate potential threats. However, his old-school approach often clashes with the modern world's nuances, forcing him to evolve his tactics and learn to work within an unfamiliar environment.

The Beginning of a New Empire

Tulsa King follows Dwight as he begins to carve out a criminal empire in Tulsa, piecing together a new crew and reasserting his authority in a town that has no existing mafia infrastructure. Unlike New York, where loyalty is often rooted in long-standing connections and unspoken agreements, Tulsa requires a different approach. Dwight must build trust from scratch, navigating a new landscape where alliances are tentative, and loyalty is not guaranteed. This journey requires him to exercise both patience and adaptability, as he cultivates relationships with a cast of colorful characters—each with their motivations, insecurities, and ambitions.

Dwight's journey in *Tulsa King* is one of resilience, adaptation, and power. Exiled to a new world yet fueled by the same loyalty and iron will that defined his past, he embarks on a mission not only to reclaim his status but to reassert his value to himself and those who may have underestimated him. He's a man of contradictions—hardened yet humorous, ruthless yet protective. As he begins this new chapter, Dwight Manfredi's story serves as a testament to the endurance of the human spirit, even in a man whose life is bound by violence, loyalty, and a code that refuses to die.

Chapter 2: The Move to Tulsa
Why Tulsa? Analyzing the Mafia's Choice of Exile for "The General"

The decision to exile Dwight "The General" Manfredi to Tulsa, Oklahoma, is more than just an odd twist in his journey; it's a move layered with intent, perhaps even contempt. When Dwight emerges from prison after 25 years of loyalty, he expects—if not a warm welcome—at least a respectful return to his life in New York. However, his mafia family's choice to send him to Tulsa is a stark reminder of his diminished standing. This isn't just relocation; it's a rejection, a relegation to a distant and foreign landscape that's utterly removed from the world Dwight knows. The decision to send him to Tulsa is both punishment and a test, reflecting the changing dynamics within the family and perhaps a desire to keep Dwight at arm's length.

Tulsa's selection as Dwight's exile location is no random choice. Far from the organized crime networks of the East Coast, Tulsa represents a blank slate, a challenging terrain with none of the established infrastructure or reliable network of allies that Dwight once commanded in New York. The family's aim is likely twofold: to keep Dwight out of their immediate reach and to challenge his ability to adapt. The unspoken message is clear: if Dwight is still of value to the organization, he'll find a way to build something new. If he fails, his influence and loyalty are no longer of use, and he'll fade into obscurity in the relative anonymity of Tulsa. For the family, this decision to exile Dwight could be seen as an act of convenience, keeping him out of their affairs without completely severing ties—a symbolic yet tangible reduction in his influence.

The Psychological Impact of Exile on Dwight

For Dwight, the move to Tulsa isn't just a shift in physical location; it's a profound blow to his identity, pride, and sense of purpose. He dedicated his life to the family, choosing prison over betrayal, sacrificing his freedom and time for the organization's well-being. But his loyalty appears to have been repaid with an act of indifference and exile, shattering any illusions of appreciation or recognition he might have clung to during his years behind bars. Dwight's initial reaction is marked by a combination of disbelief, anger, and defiance. While he's a master of self-control, the psychological toll of exile begins to weigh on him, testing his resolve as he grapples with feelings of betrayal and displacement.

There's an internal conflict that Dwight faces in Tulsa: the need to reassert his identity and worth without the familiar context of his old life. His mind constantly oscillates between wanting to prove his value by building something in Tulsa and feeling resentful toward a family that treated him as disposable. This tension is evident as he moves through his new surroundings, alternately embracing the challenge and rejecting the reality of his exile. Dwight's years in prison have toughened him, teaching him patience and adaptability, yet even he cannot escape the sting of being cast aside by the very people for whom he sacrificed everything.

Initial Reactions: Dwight's First Impressions of Tulsa

Upon arrival, Dwight is struck by the stark contrast between Tulsa and New York—a juxtaposition that almost serves as a metaphor for his current life situation. In place of the crowded skyscrapers and constant hum of the city, Tulsa presents wide-open spaces, slow-moving streets, and a sense of isolation that feels as foreign to Dwight as the technology he now must learn to use. He sees Tulsa as barren ground, a place of opportunity if handled correctly, yet the lack of a preexisting criminal network feels both liberating and disconcerting. Unlike New York, where he knew every player and every rule, Tulsa is a blank canvas, and

Dwight must both learn the lay of the land and establish his authority from scratch.

At first, Dwight's reaction to Tulsa is tinted with frustration and a touch of amusement. The city's slower pace, friendly locals, and suburban simplicity are the antithesis of his hardened urban experiences. His initial interactions with the people of Tulsa are often tinged with humor, especially as he struggles to adjust to the cultural and social differences. Dwight's attempts to navigate the town highlight his fish-out-of-water predicament, providing comic relief as he tries to apply his New York mafia tactics to a population that isn't accustomed to his way of doing things. While Dwight may view the city with a mix of derision and skepticism at first, he also recognizes that its unassuming nature provides an opportunity for a fresh start—a chance to build something uniquely his own, free from the constraints and betrayals of his old life.

Tulsa as a New Frontier for Crime

Tulsa's unassuming nature offers both advantages and challenges for a man like Dwight. While the city lacks an established criminal underworld on par with New York, this absence is also an invitation for innovation. Unlike the crowded criminal ecosystem of his past, Tulsa is an untapped market, a place where Dwight can create a new power structure without competing with established players. This possibility excites him; in Tulsa, he has a chance to shape the underworld on his own terms, to build an empire from scratch without the limitations of legacy rivalries or territorial disputes.

The potential for establishing a new criminal network in Tulsa appeals to Dwight's strategic mind. He begins by observing the landscape, identifying weaknesses and opportunities within the local community. From strip clubs and bars to gambling dens and small-time operators, Dwight sees Tulsa as a new frontier, a canvas for his skills as a leader and strategist. The town's unregulated nature and lack of organized crime offer him the perfect platform to reinvent himself, harnessing his experience to mold a criminal empire uniquely suited to the city's character. However, this lack of infrastructure also requires him to exercise patience and flexibility, traits that don't come naturally to a man used to operating within a well-oiled mafia machine.

Dwight's Determination to Prove His Value

Dwight's exile to Tulsa may be a punishment, but for him, it also becomes a test of his resilience, adaptability, and strategic prowess. Far from being defeated, Dwight views Tulsa as an opportunity to redefine his legacy. While the family may have intended his relocation as a subtle way of pushing him into obscurity, Dwight sees it as a chance to prove his worth once again. His determination to succeed is fueled by a sense of defiance, a refusal to let his loyalty and sacrifice be rendered meaningless. If he can build something powerful and profitable in Tulsa, it will serve as a statement to the family—a reminder that Dwight Manfredi is far from obsolete.

As he begins to assemble his new network, Dwight's tactics reflect a blend of old-school mafia principles and a willingness to adapt to his surroundings. He quickly realizes that the people of Tulsa require a different approach; they're not accustomed to the rough-and-tumble, loyalty-based world he's familiar with. Yet Dwight's charisma, pragmatism, and strategic mind give him a unique edge. He's a natural leader, someone who can command respect through presence alone, and as he recruits allies and builds connections, he does so with an unwavering focus on proving his value—not only to his mafia family back in New York but also to himself.

The Road Ahead: Establishing Control in a Foreign Land

The road to dominance in Tulsa won't be an easy one, but Dwight's journey is fueled by the fire of resilience and a need to prove himself. Every decision, every alliance, and every calculated risk is part of his plan to turn Tulsa into a profitable empire. Dwight's strategy is methodical, shaped by years of experience, and he quickly learns to capitalize on the town's unique character. He uses his charm and intimidation to forge alliances with local players, leveraging their skills and resources while ensuring they understand who's in charge.

As Dwight begins to make his mark on Tulsa, he's aware of the stakes—failure isn't an option. He's playing a long game, balancing short-term gains with a vision for a sustainable power base. The stakes are high, and each step Dwight takes is fraught with both opportunity and risk. Yet his resolve remains unwavering. With every small victory, he chips away at the obstacles in his path, determined to build something that will not only establish his dominance in Tulsa but also serve as a testament to his legacy and his defiance of those who cast him aside.

Conclusion: Tulsa as the Beginning of a New Chapter

For Dwight "The General" Manfredi, Tulsa isn't just a place; it's the beginning of a new chapter. Stripped of his past and cast into unfamiliar territory, Dwight faces both the challenge and opportunity of starting anew. His move to Tulsa is a pivotal moment that will redefine him as a character, a leader, and a survivor. Through this exile, Dwight is forced to confront the limits of his power, adapt to an ever-evolving world, and build a legacy that transcends betrayal and loss.

In many ways, Tulsa becomes Dwight's crucible, a place where he will either rise to new heights or be forgotten entirely. His journey is one of resilience and redemption, a testament to his unbreakable spirit and unwavering loyalty to himself. With each step he takes toward building his empire, Dwight Manfredi not only cements his place in Tulsa but also redefines what it means to be "The General"—a leader, a survivor, and a man determined to prove that exile is merely the beginning of something greater.

Chapter 3: New Beginnings in Tulsa
The First Days: Dwight's Initial Impressions of Tulsa

For Dwight "The General" Manfredi, stepping off the bus in Tulsa is a moment both jarring and humbling. It's a far cry from the towering skyline and gritty pulse of New York City, where the underworld was as much a part of the culture as Wall Street. Here in Tulsa, he finds a city marked by an unassuming charm and a slower pace, qualities that feel alien to a man who spent decades thriving in the high-stakes, fast-paced world of the East Coast mafia. The city's simplicity and relative quietness seem to taunt him, a reminder that he's been exiled from the action and power he once knew. But while Tulsa appears mundane on the surface, Dwight quickly realizes that it's a place ripe with hidden opportunities.

These first days are pivotal for Dwight. He's stripped of the familiar networks and resources he once relied upon, forced to begin at ground zero in a city that doesn't know or fear him. Dwight's observations are sharp; he notes the people's mannerisms, the local businesses, and the unspoken social dynamics. His mind, honed from years of survival and strategy, is constantly assessing and recalibrating, trying to discern the weak points and potential allies. While Tulsa may seem disorienting at first, Dwight approaches it like any other battlefield: with patience, precision, and an unwavering focus on finding his place within its social landscape.

Exploring the Local Scene

As Dwight begins to navigate Tulsa's local scene, he quickly learns that the city operates by a different set of rules. The people here are mostly small-town types, straightforward and grounded, a contrast to the streetwise operators and hardened criminals he's accustomed to dealing with. Unlike New York, where loyalty often hinges on fear or financial gain, Tulsa is a place where relationships are built on trust and familiarity, qualities that aren't readily offered to an outsider like Dwight. His first encounters with the locals reveal both the challenges and opportunities of his new environment, prompting him to adapt his tactics to fit a culture that doesn't easily bend to his style of intimidation and command.

Tulsa's nightlife is modest compared to the opulent clubs and underground bars of New York, but Dwight sees potential in its simplicity. He visits local bars, observes the regulars, and notes how business is conducted in this quieter setting. He sees potential not in the scale of these operations but in their lack of sophistication—there are no entrenched power structures here, no organized crime syndicates vying for control. This realization gives Dwight a sense of freedom and possibility. Unlike New York, where the competition is cutthroat and alliances are temporary, Tulsa presents a blank slate for him to mold as he sees fit. The challenge will be earning the respect of a populace that's more likely to be suspicious than reverent of a man like Dwight.

First Allies and Encounters

In his early days, Dwight begins scouting for potential allies, individuals who can help him establish a foothold in Tulsa. He's not looking for hardened criminals or mafia insiders—he's far from the resources and connections that would typically supply such people. Instead, he looks for locals with useful skills, people on the fringes of society who might be open to an opportunity or two that pays under the table. He visits a few of the seedier bars and local haunts, looking for those whose loyalty can be bought, won, or inspired by his presence and promises.

One of Dwight's first allies is a local bar owner named Bodhi, a low-key but resourceful figure with connections in the town's more discreet circles. Bodhi becomes a valuable asset, providing Dwight with a first-hand understanding of the city's underground economy. As a small-time operator with a touch of ambition, Bodhi is intrigued by Dwight's proposition to make money outside the law, though he remains wary of the implications. For Dwight, Bodhi represents both an entry point into Tulsa's local scene and an example of the type of ally he'll need to find success in this foreign environment.

Through Bodhi, Dwight is introduced to a few other Tulsa locals who might be open to bending the rules. Among them are a mechanic who occasionally deals in stolen car parts, a low-level dealer who supplies the local college crowd, and a few other small-time players. These aren't hardened gangsters, but they offer Dwight the connections he needs to begin piecing together a network. He understands that building loyalty with these people will require a softer approach, so he emphasizes the potential for profits and stability that come with his presence in town.

Learning the Lay of the Land: Tulsa's Social and Criminal Landscape

Tulsa's social dynamics are different from New York's. Here, community ties run deep, and people are suspicious of outsiders. Dwight learns quickly that if he wants to make a mark, he'll need to work within these social frameworks, adapting his tactics to fit a place where reputation and respect matter as much as, if not more than, fear. The local businesses are all owned and run by people who've known each other for years, and his typical approach of intimidation and dominance won't win him the alliances he needs.

In addition to the social dynamics, Dwight begins to map out the criminal landscape, limited as it may be. There's no major criminal organization in Tulsa; rather, it's a patchwork of small-time hustlers, petty dealers, and the occasional biker gang. This lack of centralized power means that, with the right moves, Dwight could unify these fragmented elements under his control. But he knows that achieving this will require patience, subtlety, and a level of charm he's not accustomed to using. By understanding these dynamics, Dwight identifies the gaps in Tulsa's underworld—the spaces where he can establish control and bring organization to what is currently a disorganized and low-stakes criminal scene.

Establishing Control: Early Moves and Strategic Planning

In his first few days, Dwight begins to lay the groundwork for his operations in Tulsa. He knows that establishing control won't happen overnight, so he starts by making small moves, testing the waters to see how the locals react. His strategy is careful and calculated; rather than asserting his dominance outright, he starts by building relationships, earning the trust of a few key figures, and showing people the value of having a man like him around.

Dwight's first order of business is to establish a profitable venture that can serve as both a front and a revenue stream. Through Bodhi and his connections, he learns about the possibility of running a cannabis operation—a business that, while semi-legal, has enough gray areas to allow for off-the-books profit. Dwight sees this as a perfect fit for his initial plans: it's lucrative, relatively low-risk, and can operate under the radar without drawing too much attention from law enforcement. His initial conversations with Bodhi and others in the local scene focus on organizing this business, creating a discreet operation that will offer him both financial security and a foundation for his expanding network.

As Dwight starts setting up this operation, he exercises caution in his dealings with law enforcement. He knows from experience that no criminal enterprise can survive without a careful balance of power and influence, so he makes a point of learning about Tulsa's local police force and identifying individuals who might be open to an "understanding." This process is delicate, requiring a blend of subtle intimidation and diplomatic charm. Dwight is mindful of not overstepping too early, aware that his presence in Tulsa is already bound to raise eyebrows among both the locals and the police.

Winning Respect and Building a Reputation

From the moment Dwight arrived in Tulsa, he understood that his success depended on more than just setting up a profitable business—it required earning respect and building a reputation. In New York, his title and history would have been enough to command both fear and loyalty. But here in Tulsa, he's an unknown quantity, an outsider whose intentions are not yet trusted or understood. He realizes that if he wants to be taken seriously, he'll need to prove himself through actions, not just words.

One of Dwight's earliest moves to establish his reputation is to quietly intervene in a local dispute. When one of his new contacts faces harassment from a rival, Dwight steps in, using his presence and a few well-placed threats to diffuse the situation. The gesture is calculated; he isn't seeking outright conflict but rather aiming to show the locals that he's both capable and willing to protect those who align with him. This act of protection, while subtle, earns him a degree of respect from those who witness it, laying the groundwork for future alliances.

Over the next few days, Dwight makes a point of showing the locals what he can offer—stability, protection, and a level of profitability they haven't experienced before. He refrains from asserting control too aggressively, opting instead to gain people's trust by demonstrating his value. His approach is a mixture of confidence and caution, recognizing that his power in Tulsa will ultimately depend on the willingness of others to stand with him.

Setting the Foundation for a New Empire

As Dwight wraps up his first days in Tulsa, he's already begun to lay the foundation for what he envisions as a new criminal empire. Though the process is slow, he can feel the momentum building, a sense of control and purpose taking shape as he earns the trust of locals and recruits allies. The small successes he's achieved in just a few days fuel his drive to go further, to expand his operations and bring his vision to fruition.

Dwight's early moves in Tulsa aren't just about profit—they're about establishing a base of operations that he can grow over time. His plans are expansive, and he knows that the cannabis operation is only the beginning. As his influence grows, he envisions branching out, creating a network that will allow him to control multiple streams of revenue and protect his territory from any rivals who may arise. For Dwight, each step forward is a testament to his resilience, his adaptability, and his relentless pursuit of power and respect.

Conclusion: The Path to Power

In these first days, Dwight Manfredi is not merely finding his footing in Tulsa; he's staking his claim, building a foundation for what he hopes will become a thriving empire. He has faced the initial challenges of navigating an unfamiliar environment, finding allies, and laying down roots—all while adapting his methods to suit the slower pace and cautious nature of Tulsa's local scene. His journey is just beginning, and with every calculated move, he solidifies his place in the city's shadowy underworld.

As Dwight takes his first steps toward establishing control in Tulsa, he's keenly aware of the journey ahead. The path will be challenging, filled with obstacles and risks, but he's undeterred. Fueled by a desire to prove himself, reclaim his status, and build something that no one can take from him, Dwight Manfredi is ready to turn Tulsa into a kingdom worthy of a general—one brick, one ally, and one victory at a time.

Chapter 4: Establishing Power in an Unfamiliar Land
The Challenge of Building a Criminal Empire from Scratch

Establishing a criminal enterprise is a feat under the best of circumstances, but for Dwight "The General" Manfredi, doing so in Tulsa—a city that is largely untouched by the organized crime scene he once dominated—requires a blend of patience, intelligence, and adaptability. Dwight enters Tulsa with nothing but his instincts and experience, forced to build a new network of allies, loyalists, and business fronts in a city where his reputation means little. While he's no stranger to navigating the complexities of power, he's keenly aware that this isn't New York. There are no established structures or reliable contacts to fall back on, and the cultural nuances of Tulsa present unique challenges. Here, relationships are built slowly, based on trust, and reputations are earned over time, not through sheer intimidation alone.

Dwight knows he's up against two key hurdles: his outsider status and the lack of an existing criminal framework that he can simply step into. He must create something from scratch while ensuring that he doesn't draw unnecessary attention from law enforcement or provoke the locals into hostility. This chapter of Dwight's journey is marked by strategic planning, careful recruitment, and calculated risks as he sets out to build a criminal empire suited to Tulsa's distinct environment. His methods blend traditional mob tactics with new approaches that take into account the idiosyncrasies of a place where people are often wary of strangers and prefer community bonds over fear-based loyalty.

Step 1: Securing a Financial Base

For Dwight, establishing a steady stream of income is the first priority. Without money, he can't secure influence, pay off law enforcement, or support the loyalists he hopes to gather. He begins with a pragmatic approach, deciding to leverage the semi-legal cannabis industry as the backbone of his initial operation. Cannabis offers a unique opportunity; it's lucrative and, while technically legal, remains an area filled with gray-market opportunities. Dwight's plan is to start a cannabis distribution network, operating in a semi-legal space where he can maximize profits while keeping a low profile.

To set up this operation, Dwight taps into his budding network, recruiting Bodhi, the local bar owner, as both an ally and business partner. Bodhi's knowledge of the local economy and his ability to navigate Tulsa's social scene make him invaluable, and Dwight uses their partnership as a stepping stone to establish his cannabis operation. Together, they form a discreet distribution network, utilizing Bodhi's bar as a base for product exchanges and transactions. Dwight meticulously ensures that everything operates under the radar, avoiding flashy moves or high-risk stunts that might attract unwanted attention. This venture isn't just a cash cow; it's the foundation of Dwight's power in Tulsa, providing both the funds and influence he'll need to expand further.

Step 2: Building Alliances and Earning Trust

Dwight's second order of business is to expand his network of allies. He recognizes that in Tulsa, where loyalty is built slowly and relationships matter, his traditional mafia tactics of intimidation and fear won't get him very far. Instead, he adopts a more nuanced approach, seeking to earn respect and trust rather than simply demanding obedience. Each alliance he forms is carefully considered, with Dwight prioritizing individuals who are well-connected within the community and capable of providing useful skills or resources.

His recruitment efforts lead him to engage with a variety of Tulsa locals, each with a unique set of talents and connections. One of these is Mitch, a local mechanic with a reputation for discretion and a sideline in stolen car parts. Mitch becomes Dwight's go-to man for transport and logistics, helping him move products quietly and offering repair services that can double as a way to launder money. In Dwight's mind, Mitch represents the practical, blue-collar approach to crime that's needed in Tulsa—he's reliable, low-profile, and operates in a space where his actions are less likely to draw scrutiny.

Another key alliance is with Tina, a mid-level dealer who has her finger on the pulse of Tulsa's college scene. Tina's small-time operation serves as Dwight's entry point into a younger demographic, providing him with both new customers and additional distribution channels. Dwight approaches her carefully, recognizing that she's skeptical of his motives as an outsider. Instead of attempting to muscle his way in, Dwight offers Tina a mutually beneficial arrangement: he'll protect her and supply her at a lower cost, allowing her to expand her operation while giving him access to her clientele. This strategic partnership highlights Dwight's adaptability; rather than forcing control, he empowers Tina, making her more loyal and invested in his enterprise.

Step 3: Navigating Enemies and Rivals

No empire-building process is without its challenges, and Dwight's journey is no exception. His presence in Tulsa doesn't go unnoticed, and as he begins to expand his influence, he inevitably attracts the attention of those who feel threatened by his arrival. Among them are local small-time operators who see Dwight as a threat to their territory and control, as well as law enforcement officers who are suspicious of the new face in town and eager to prove their vigilance.

One of Dwight's early rivals is Red, a mid-level biker with connections to a local motorcycle gang that has a loose grip on parts of Tulsa's criminal activity. Red is used to operating without interference and views Dwight's cannabis operation as an encroachment on his territory. Their initial encounters are tense, with Red testing Dwight's resolve by sending thinly veiled threats and attempting to intimidate Bodhi. However, Dwight isn't easily rattled; rather than responding with brute force, he handles the situation with a cool, calculated approach. He arranges a "meeting" with Red, using his charisma and assertiveness to convey that he's not here to cause trouble—unless trouble is brought to him. This encounter establishes Dwight's reputation as someone who is calm under pressure but won't tolerate disrespect.

Through his interactions with Red and other rivals, Dwight establishes a balance between intimidation and diplomacy, carefully choosing when to assert his dominance and when to step back. He recognizes that overt aggression could lead to unnecessary conflict, so he carefully navigates these tensions, ensuring that his rivals understand his power without directly provoking them. Over time, his handling of these situations builds his reputation as a strategic operator—someone who can be respected, but not easily crossed.

Step 4: Asserting Influence in the Community

Dwight's approach to power in Tulsa goes beyond criminal alliances; he's keenly aware that establishing influence within the broader community is essential. Unlike New York, where fear and reputation were often sufficient, Tulsa requires a different tactic. Dwight begins to insert himself into local spaces, attending community events, frequenting local businesses, and ensuring that people recognize him not as a shadowy outsider but as someone who belongs. His involvement is carefully managed; he shows genuine interest in the community, making small donations to local causes and offering support to neighborhood initiatives. By becoming a familiar face, Dwight begins to shift public perception, slowly building an image as a well-meaning businessman rather than a dangerous criminal.

This community-focused approach also serves a practical purpose: it provides Dwight with a safety net. By ingratiating himself with the locals, he gains a certain level of protection from law enforcement and reduces the likelihood of neighbors reporting suspicious activities. He knows that if he can make himself valuable to the community, people will be less inclined to view him as a threat, and in some cases, may even protect him out of gratitude or respect. This tactic proves effective, as locals start to see Dwight as a man with a genuine interest in Tulsa's well-being, blurring the line between criminal enterprise and community involvement.

Step 5: Establishing Control Over Law Enforcement

Dwight knows that any criminal enterprise is only as strong as its protection from law enforcement. He's no stranger to the delicate art of handling police and recognizes that, in Tulsa, a subtle approach is necessary. Rather than attempting to bribe officers directly, he begins by identifying individuals within the local law enforcement who may be open to a mutually beneficial arrangement. His interactions with the police are carefully managed, and he opts for a cautious approach, recognizing that a heavy-handed tactic could backfire in a community as tightly knit as Tulsa.

Through discrete conversations and indirect channels, Dwight learns about the officers who might be willing to look the other way. He approaches them not with threats but with offers of financial assistance and reassurances that his presence in Tulsa is beneficial to the community. Over time, he secures a few allies within the force, individuals who are willing to overlook minor infractions in exchange for a steady stream of income. This arrangement provides Dwight with a crucial layer of security, allowing him to operate with relative impunity while maintaining the appearance of legitimacy.

The Rise of Dwight's Empire in Tulsa

As Dwight's alliances deepen and his revenue streams stabilize, his operation begins to take on the shape of a full-fledged criminal empire. He has established a base of loyal allies, diversified his income through cannabis and small-time protection rackets, and cultivated a reputation that makes people both respect and fear him. His influence spreads slowly but steadily, reaching into various aspects of Tulsa's underworld and beyond, creating a network that blends criminal activities with a semblance of community respectability.

Each step Dwight takes brings him closer to solidifying his control over Tulsa. He's no longer the exiled mafia capo with nothing to his name—he's becoming a powerful figure in his own right, someone whose influence is felt across the city. The cannabis operation grows, attracting a steady flow of cash, and Dwight's protective services give him an edge in the local economy, ensuring that those under his wing remain loyal and protected. His enemies may still linger, but they now tread carefully, recognizing that Dwight is not someone to be underestimated.

Conclusion: A New King in Tulsa

By the end of these early months, Dwight has established himself as a formidable presence in Tulsa. He has built a criminal empire that, while smaller in scale than his former life in New York, is uniquely suited to Tulsa's landscape and character. His influence extends beyond the realm of crime, reaching into the community and creating a network of respect, loyalty, and calculated power. Through strategic alliances, thoughtful community involvement, and careful management of both allies and enemies, Dwight has created a foundation for something far greater.

This chapter marks the beginning of Dwight's transformation from an exiled outsider to a respected—and feared—kingpin in Tulsa. His journey is far from over, and challenges still loom on the horizon, but he's proven that his resilience and strategic mind are as sharp as ever. With a foothold in the city and an expanding empire, Dwight Manfredi is ready to make Tulsa his own, a kingdom where he reigns supreme in a place that once sought to strip him of his power.

Chapter 5: Stallone's Performance: A Deep Dive
Introduction: Stallone as "The General"

Sylvester Stallone's portrayal of Dwight "The General" Manfredi in *Tulsa King* is a masterclass in embodying a character who is as tough as he is nuanced. Known for his iconic roles as rugged, often misunderstood anti-heroes in films like *Demolition Man* and *Judge Dredd*, Stallone brings a familiar intensity to the screen but tempers it with layers of vulnerability and humor that elevate his performance. In *Tulsa King*, Stallone captures the essence of a man wrestling with his legacy, his principles, and the reality of starting anew in a world he barely recognizes. Stallone's Dwight is not just a criminal mastermind; he is a man shaped by loyalty, sacrifice, and the hardened resilience born from spending 25 years behind bars.

What makes Stallone's portrayal of Dwight so compelling is the blend of physicality and emotional depth he brings to the role. Stallone, who has long been celebrated for his commanding on-screen presence, uses his iconic toughness to embody Dwight's inner conflict—balancing brute force with introspection and strategic calculation. In this chapter, we'll explore how Stallone's performance in *Tulsa King* echoes his past roles in *Demolition Man* and *Judge Dredd* while marking a new evolution in his acting, showcasing his ability to transform an archetypal mob figure into a layered character driven by both ambition and existential reflection.

Physicality and Presence: A Toughness Reminiscent of *Demolition Man* and *Judge Dredd*

Stallone's portrayal of Dwight draws heavily on the physicality that has become his trademark. Much like his roles as John Spartan in *Demolition Man* and the titular character in *Judge Dredd*, Stallone commands attention with his physical presence. In both films, he plays characters defined by their resilience, toughness, and almost mythic status as enforcers of justice (albeit through different lenses). In *Tulsa King*, however, this physicality is recontextualized to reflect Dwight's age, weariness, and experience, offering a more grounded version of the power and authority Stallone brought to these earlier roles.

In *Demolition Man*, Stallone's character, John Spartan, was a cop unfrozen in a future that no longer adhered to his violent, no-nonsense approach to crime-fighting. Similarly, *Judge Dredd* presented him as a near-invincible lawman bound by an unyielding code of justice in a dystopian society. In both cases, Stallone's characters used their physical dominance to assert control over chaotic environments. With Dwight, Stallone conveys that same underlying strength, but he tempers it with age and subtle restraint. Dwight doesn't charge in guns blazing; instead, he's a man whose sheer presence and reputation often do the talking before he needs to lift a finger. Stallone uses his physicality as an unspoken language, showing Dwight's power not through overt violence but through a steady, calculated approach to confrontation.

Even Dwight's body language—the confident yet measured way he walks, the slow, deliberate gestures, and the calculating gaze—speaks to a character who has lived through hardships and learned to conserve his energy. Unlike the kinetic action sequences of *Demolition Man* and *Judge Dredd*, Stallone's performance in *Tulsa King* relies on small, intentional movements, reflecting a character who knows the importance of picking his battles. This subtle physicality allows Stallone to embody

Dwight's complex personality, using restraint and focus to create a character who is as intimidating as he is introspective.

Depth and Vulnerability: The Aging Anti-Hero

Stallone's performance as Dwight marks an evolution in his portrayal of the anti-hero, moving beyond the purely physical and exploring the vulnerabilities of a man facing his twilight years. Unlike *Demolition Man* and *Judge Dredd*, where Stallone's characters were almost superhuman enforcers bound to their missions, Dwight is a deeply flawed, introspective figure grappling with the weight of lost time and the challenges of adapting to a world that has moved on without him. Stallone taps into this vulnerability, giving Dwight an emotional depth that wasn't as evident in his earlier roles.

Dwight's age and experience manifest as a kind of quiet sadness, a regretful acceptance of all he has lost in the 25 years he spent in prison. Stallone captures this through subtle expressions—a fleeting look of weariness, a sigh heavy with unspoken memories, or a reflective silence after a conversation. Unlike the unyielding characters he played in his youth, Stallone's Dwight is visibly haunted by his past and wary of his future. This sense of vulnerability is one of the most captivating aspects of Stallone's performance, making Dwight not just a mobster but a man searching for purpose, redemption, and meaning in a life defined by sacrifice and loss.

The quiet moments where Dwight reflects on his past—either through a conversation or a simple gaze into the distance—allow Stallone to showcase a depth of emotion that resonates with viewers. He transforms Dwight into a character who, despite his rough edges and criminal tendencies, elicits empathy. Stallone's ability to imbue Dwight with this vulnerability adds layers to the performance, creating a sense of complexity that elevates Dwight from a stereotypical mob figure to a multidimensional man.

Humor and Humanity: A New Layer in Stallone's Acting

One of the standout elements of Stallone's performance in *Tulsa King* is the humor he brings to Dwight's character. While *Demolition Man* featured comedic elements through Stallone's interactions with a future society, and *Judge Dredd* allowed for moments of dark wit, *Tulsa King* fully embraces humor as part of Dwight's character. Stallone uses humor not as a distraction but as a means of humanizing Dwight, allowing him to connect with both the locals in Tulsa and the audience in a way that feels genuine.

Dwight's humor often arises from his attempts to navigate a modern world filled with technology, social changes, and cultural shifts that are entirely foreign to him. Stallone's portrayal of these moments is both comedic and endearing, as Dwight struggles with smartphones, slang, and social media. Rather than relying on slapstick, Stallone's humor is dry and understated, often conveyed through deadpan delivery or a bemused expression. This comedic timing adds a refreshing layer to the character, making Dwight more relatable and likable, even as he pursues morally ambiguous goals.

Through these moments of humor, Stallone conveys Dwight's adaptability, resourcefulness, and willingness to learn, qualities that make him more than just a hardened mobster. The humor adds a softness to Dwight's character, revealing a man who, despite his reputation and criminal background, possesses a keen sense of irony and an openness to change. Stallone's ability to balance this humor with Dwight's toughness and vulnerability makes his performance uniquely memorable, allowing viewers to see Dwight as a character with depth, wit, and humanity.

Commanding Authority and Leadership: The Mob Boss Redefined

Stallone's portrayal of Dwight "The General" as a leader is another notable aspect of his performance, setting him apart from the traditional mob boss archetype. In *Demolition Man* and *Judge Dredd*, Stallone's characters commanded authority through sheer force, imposing their will on others with an almost robotic sense of duty. In *Tulsa King*, however, Stallone brings a different kind of authority to Dwight—one built on respect, loyalty, and strategic intelligence. Rather than relying on fear alone, Dwight earns his followers' respect through his loyalty, experience, and willingness to protect those who stand by him.

Stallone infuses Dwight with a unique sense of leadership, portraying him as someone who understands the value of loyalty and mutual respect. Dwight doesn't demand allegiance; he inspires it, showing his followers that he values them as individuals rather than mere assets. Stallone's portrayal of this leadership style highlights Dwight's evolution as a character, reflecting a man who has learned the importance of treating people as equals rather than subordinates. This approach to leadership is a refreshing departure from the ruthless mob boss stereotype, giving Dwight a sense of nobility that makes him both a feared and respected figure.

Through Stallone's nuanced performance, Dwight becomes a character who balances empathy with toughness, showing his followers that he is willing to fight for them as long as they remain loyal. This sense of honor and loyalty resonates throughout Stallone's portrayal, reinforcing Dwight's reputation as "The General" not only in name but in spirit. Stallone captures the essence of a leader who is both feared and respected, creating a character who commands loyalty through his actions and integrity rather than through threats and intimidation alone.

Stallone's Signature Style: Blending Action with Emotional Depth

Stallone's unique ability to blend action with emotional complexity is one of the defining features of his portrayal of Dwight. While *Demolition Man* and *Judge Dredd* were action-driven, focusing primarily on Stallone's prowess in combat and his stoic approach to justice, *Tulsa King* allows him to explore a more subdued form of action, one that is intertwined with Dwight's personal struggles and emotional journey. Stallone's Dwight doesn't rely solely on physical confrontations; instead, he uses his wit, charisma, and strategic mind to navigate conflict, making every decision with an awareness of the broader consequences.

When Dwight does engage in physical altercations, Stallone's portrayal emphasizes precision and restraint. Each fight is calculated, serving a purpose rather than being a gratuitous display of violence. This approach reflects Dwight's age, experience, and understanding of power. He no longer fights to prove himself; he fights only when necessary. Stallone's nuanced handling of these scenes adds gravity to each confrontation, making Dwight's actions feel meaningful and impactful. Through this balance of action and introspection, Stallone brings a new layer to his performance, showing viewers that Dwight is a character who fights not out of compulsion but as a means of survival and assertion of control.

Conclusion: A Role That Bridges Stallone's Past and Present

Sylvester Stallone's portrayal of Dwight Manfredi in *Tulsa King* is a testament to his growth as an actor, blending the toughness and charisma that defined his earlier roles with a newfound vulnerability and emotional depth. Through Dwight, Stallone revisits the themes of loyalty, resilience, and leadership that marked his work in *Demolition Man* and *Judge Dredd*, but he infuses these traits with a wisdom and introspection that reflect his own evolution as both an actor and a storyteller.

In *Tulsa King*, Stallone creates a character who is as complex as he is commanding, embodying the contradictions of a man who is both ruthless and compassionate, weary yet driven. Dwight is a character who resonates with audiences not just because of his power or presence but because of his humanity—a testament to Stallone's ability to transform an archetype into a fully realized, multidimensional figure. Stallone's performance as Dwight "The General" Manfredi is more than just a continuation of his legacy as an action star; it's a reimagining of what it means to be a leader, a survivor, and, ultimately, a man searching for redemption in a world that has left him behind.

Chapter 6: The Supporting Cast
Introduction: A World Built Around "The General"

While Dwight "The General" Manfredi, portrayed by Sylvester Stallone, is the centerpiece of *Tulsa King*, the supporting cast plays an integral role in shaping both the narrative and Dwight's character arc. The individuals who orbit around Dwight offer diverse perspectives and motivations, contributing layers of complexity to the story and allowing viewers to experience Tulsa through a spectrum of personalities, loyalties, and conflicts. Each supporting character brings a unique set of strengths, weaknesses, and backgrounds that help Dwight navigate, adapt, and ultimately establish his power in Tulsa. This ensemble enriches the storyline by challenging Dwight's values, testing his patience, and providing him with alliances and obstacles that reveal new facets of his personality and ambition.

In this chapter, we'll explore the key characters surrounding Dwight, examining their backgrounds, motivations, and relationships with "The General." Through these relationships, we see Dwight's vulnerabilities, his strategic thinking, and his capacity for both ruthless pragmatism and unexpected compassion. The supporting cast not only adds depth to Dwight's journey but also brings vibrancy to the world of *Tulsa King*, grounding the narrative in a complex social web that reflects the gritty reality of survival, loyalty, and ambition in the underworld.

Bodhi: The Local Bar Owner and Trusted Confidant

Bodhi is one of the first people Dwight connects with upon his arrival in Tulsa, a local bar owner with his own set of resources and a discreet presence in the city's nightlife. Bodhi's bar serves as a neutral ground—a place where various figures of Tulsa's underworld come and go, providing Dwight with a valuable vantage point for observing the city's social dynamics. Bodhi is somewhat reserved but possesses a quiet intelligence, blending a sense of wariness with a curiosity about Dwight and his plans for Tulsa. His experience running a local business gives him an understanding of the community, as well as a level of influence that Dwight recognizes and seeks to leverage.

As the story unfolds, Bodhi's role evolves from a simple business partner to one of Dwight's most trusted confidants. His connections within Tulsa's low-profile circles prove invaluable as Dwight seeks to expand his operations discreetly. Although Bodhi is initially skeptical of Dwight's motives, he quickly realizes that aligning himself with "The General" could elevate his own status and provide security in a volatile environment. Bodhi's skepticism also keeps Dwight grounded, serving as a moral compass and often questioning Dwight's methods, which provides a subtle tension that enriches their dynamic. Through Bodhi, we see Dwight's willingness to listen, adjust, and even compromise, showcasing his adaptability and understanding of the importance of local support.

Mitch: The Mechanic and Loyal Ally

Mitch, a skilled mechanic with a sideline in less-than-legal business dealings, becomes a critical part of Dwight's new empire. His shop serves as a base of operations for handling logistics, repairs, and transportation, giving Dwight the infrastructure he needs to move products and people around the city. Mitch is a rough-around-the-edges character with a pragmatic approach to life, and he shares Dwight's desire to keep things under the radar while ensuring they're profitable. Unlike some of the other locals, Mitch is quick to recognize Dwight's potential and respects his experience, seeing him as a figure who can bring order to Tulsa's fragmented underworld.

Mitch's mechanical skills and discretion make him invaluable to Dwight's operation, particularly as they begin setting up the cannabis distribution network. Beyond logistics, Mitch's loyalty to Dwight is cemented early on, as he appreciates Dwight's straightforward, no-nonsense approach to leadership. This loyalty is mutual, with Dwight recognizing Mitch as one of the few people in Tulsa who he can rely on without reservation. Mitch's reliability and skill provide Dwight with a stable foundation, allowing him to expand his operations with a trusted ally by his side. Through Mitch, the series highlights Dwight's ability to build loyalty through respect and mutual benefit rather than coercion alone, adding a sense of camaraderie to Dwight's network.

Tina: The Dealer with Street Smarts

Tina, a mid-level dealer in Tulsa's college scene, represents a younger, more independent figure in Dwight's world. She's street-smart, resourceful, and cautious, qualities that have allowed her to establish a successful operation catering to a specific demographic. When Dwight approaches Tina to expand his cannabis network, she's initially wary, viewing him as an outsider whose arrival threatens her business and autonomy. However, Dwight recognizes her potential and approaches her with respect, offering protection and a better supply chain rather than attempting to take over her operation outright.

Tina's involvement with Dwight's network brings a new dimension to his operation, connecting him to a younger clientele and expanding his influence into new social circles. Her wariness keeps Dwight on his toes, reminding him that trust and respect are earned, not taken. Through her, Dwight is forced to adopt a collaborative approach, treating Tina as an equal partner rather than a subordinate. This partnership serves as a reflection of Dwight's adaptability; unlike his past life in New York, where hierarchy and control were paramount, Tulsa requires him to take a more inclusive approach. Tina's presence also adds a layer of tension, as her independent streak occasionally clashes with Dwight's methods, creating a dynamic that's both cooperative and competitive.

Stacy: The Law Enforcement Connection

Stacy is a local police officer with a keen sense of the underworld in Tulsa. Her position places her in the delicate space between upholding the law and dealing with the realities of the city's criminal elements. When she crosses paths with Dwight, she's initially suspicious, recognizing the potential disruption his arrival brings to Tulsa's relatively quiet scene. However, as Dwight begins establishing his influence in Tulsa, Stacy finds herself caught between her duty as an officer and the recognition that Dwight could bring stability to an otherwise disorganized criminal landscape.

Stacy's relationship with Dwight is complex, marked by both respect and mutual caution. She sees Dwight as a necessary evil, someone who can impose order on Tulsa's underworld without resorting to chaotic violence. While she doesn't openly endorse his actions, she understands that his presence could help her manage the city's criminal activity in a way that reduces open conflict and keeps more dangerous elements in check. For Dwight, Stacy represents both a challenge and an opportunity. He's acutely aware that her position in law enforcement could jeopardize his operation, but he also sees potential in maintaining an unspoken alliance with her. Their dynamic is characterized by subtle exchanges and unspoken understandings, as each recognizes the other's role in maintaining a precarious balance within Tulsa's criminal ecosystem.

Through Stacy, the series explores Dwight's strategic mind and his ability to navigate relationships with law enforcement. Rather than attempting to dominate or threaten her, Dwight approaches Stacy with respect and discretion, understanding that her cooperation—or at least her neutrality—will be critical to his long-term success in Tulsa. Stacy's presence also highlights the moral ambiguity of Dwight's actions, as he operates in a gray area that challenges traditional notions of right and wrong.

Armand: The Local Enforcer and Reluctant Rival

Armand is a low-level enforcer and part-time dealer who sees Dwight as both a threat and a potential ally. Used to operating in Tulsa without serious competition, Armand views Dwight's arrival as a disruption to his routine, sparking a rivalry rooted more in territorial instincts than genuine enmity. Armand is tough but lacks the strategic mindset that Dwight possesses, making him a formidable physical presence but a weaker player in the broader game of influence and power. His relationship with Dwight oscillates between rivalry and reluctant cooperation, as he begins to recognize that opposing "The General" could be detrimental to his survival.

Despite their occasional conflicts, Armand comes to appreciate Dwight's vision and strategic prowess, recognizing that aligning with him could bring more profit and stability than maintaining the status quo. However, he's not quick to relinquish his independence and occasionally tests Dwight's patience, leading to tension-filled encounters. Through Armand, Dwight faces the challenge of dealing with figures who value control and dominance over loyalty. Armand's presence also serves as a reminder of the violence that always lingers beneath the surface, as he frequently tests Dwight's authority, forcing him to assert his dominance in ways that underscore the ruthlessness needed to maintain power.

Armand's role adds an element of volatility to the story, as his unpredictable nature and reluctance to fully submit to Dwight's control introduce a tension that keeps Dwight on guard. This relationship ultimately serves as a proving ground for Dwight's authority, illustrating his ability to handle opposition and assert control without succumbing to unnecessary violence. Through Armand, *Tulsa King* highlights the fine line Dwight walks between respect and fear, showing that true power requires balancing intimidation with a sense of fairness.

Red: The Biker Gang Leader and Dwight's Major Threat

Red is the leader of a local biker gang with established influence in Tulsa's underworld, representing a significant threat to Dwight's operation. Unlike the smaller players in Tulsa, Red commands a group of loyal followers who are fiercely protective of their territory and revenue streams. He sees Dwight as an interloper, someone whose presence jeopardizes his authority and income, particularly as Dwight's cannabis operation begins encroaching on his turf. Red's approach to power is far more brutal than Dwight's, relying on intimidation and violence to maintain control, and he has little patience for negotiations or compromises.

Their relationship is fraught with tension from the start, with Red viewing Dwight as a direct competitor and potential enemy. Unlike the smaller rivals Dwight encounters, Red's gang has the resources and manpower to pose a serious challenge, forcing Dwight to adopt a cautious and strategic approach in handling this rivalry. Dwight recognizes that an outright conflict with Red would draw unwanted attention from law enforcement and destabilize the underworld dynamics he's carefully cultivated. As a result, he approaches Red with both caution and calculation, using diplomacy where possible but prepared to exert force if necessary.

Through Red, *Tulsa King* presents Dwight's most significant test in his quest for control. Red's gang challenges Dwight's authority and disrupts his operations, representing a clash of two different leadership styles—Red's reliance on fear versus Dwight's emphasis on loyalty and strategy. Their confrontations add a layer of suspense to the story, as viewers witness Dwight navigate the complexities of power in a world where alliances can shift in an instant. Red's character also adds a sense of urgency, as his presence serves as a reminder that Dwight's rise to power in Tulsa is not without formidable obstacles.

Conclusion: A Cast of Complex Relationships

The supporting characters in *Tulsa King* are not merely secondary players; they are essential components of Dwight Manfredi's journey in Tulsa. Each one brings a unique perspective, creating a dynamic social environment that challenges and enhances Dwight's character. Through these relationships, we see Dwight's adaptability, patience, and determination as he builds his empire in a city that resists easy control. These characters are more than just allies or rivals—they are reflections of the challenges and choices Dwight faces, forcing him to confront his values, his loyalty, and his ambition.

In *Tulsa King*, the supporting cast contributes as much to the story as Dwight himself, adding layers of conflict, camaraderie, and complexity to his journey. Whether they are loyal allies like Bodhi and Mitch, cautious collaborators like Tina and Stacy, or challenging rivals like Armand and Red, each character shapes the narrative, testing Dwight's resolve and influencing his path. Through them, we see a fuller picture of Dwight, not just as a mobster but as a man navigating a world of shifting loyalties, moral ambiguity, and the ever-present struggle for power.

Chapter 7: Blending Action and Humor
Introduction: A Unique Tonal Balance

One of the standout features of *Tulsa King* is its ability to seamlessly blend thrilling action with humor, creating a dynamic and engaging viewing experience. This balance between intense, high-stakes moments and comedic relief is no small feat, as both genres require distinct approaches and timing. Yet, *Tulsa King* manages to harmonize these elements, making it a show that captivates viewers through pulse-pounding sequences while inviting laughter and levity to break the tension. This tonal balance is more than just an entertaining choice; it's a reflection of Dwight Manfredi's character, who must navigate a dangerous criminal landscape while dealing with the culture shock and quirks of a new city.

Through Dwight's journey, the show explores the absurdity of his situation, emphasizing the juxtaposition of a hardened New York mob capo navigating a slower, simpler Tulsa environment. This setup allows for organic moments of humor, as Dwight tries to assert control in a world that often doesn't respond to his usual tactics. At the same time, the action scenes remain intense and gritty, reminding viewers of the inherent danger in Dwight's line of work. In this chapter, we'll explore how *Tulsa King* combines action and humor to create a unique storytelling style, examining the role each element plays in shaping the series and enhancing the viewer's experience.

The Role of Action: High-Stakes Moments That Define the Tone

In *Tulsa King*, action sequences are more than just spectacles; they're key moments that drive the narrative forward and reveal Dwight's skill, adaptability, and strategic mind. Each scene is carefully crafted to showcase Dwight's experience and strength, while also emphasizing the risks and challenges of his new life in Tulsa. The show's approach to action is grounded, reflecting Dwight's age, his pragmatism, and his ability to calculate risk before striking. Unlike younger, more impulsive characters, Dwight's physical confrontations are efficient and deliberate, driven by necessity rather than gratuitous violence.

From his early encounters with local rivals to his confrontations with biker gangs and law enforcement, each action scene is designed to reinforce Dwight's status as a force to be reckoned with, even in a city where he is an outsider. In these moments, Stallone's physicality shines, as he portrays Dwight as someone who relies on both brute force and strategy. Action sequences are choreographed with a sense of realism, capturing the grit and danger of Dwight's lifestyle. This grounding keeps the action tense and believable, making each sequence feel consequential and reinforcing the high-stakes environment Dwight operates within.

Beyond entertainment, the action sequences in *Tulsa King* serve as a character study. Through each confrontation, we see Dwight's restraint, his adherence to a code, and his understanding of when violence is warranted. His age and experience inform his approach to combat, revealing a man who knows his limits and exercises caution. This approach distinguishes *Tulsa King* from typical action dramas, as the scenes are less about showcasing flashy moves and more about underscoring Dwight's intelligence and ability to control a situation with minimal force.

Humor as a Counterbalance: Moments of Levity Amid Tension

While action grounds the show in suspense and intensity, humor provides a refreshing counterbalance that humanizes the characters and makes the storyline more relatable. *Tulsa King* uses humor to showcase the absurdity and challenges of Dwight's situation—a former New York mafia capo thrust into a small, unassuming Midwestern city where his typical tactics don't always apply. The humor arises naturally from Dwight's attempts to adapt to this new world, from his struggles with technology to his interactions with locals who are often baffled by his brusque mannerisms.

The show excels at finding humor in the details, often presenting situations that highlight Dwight's fish-out-of-water experience. For instance, Dwight's initial confusion with smartphones and social media is both humorous and endearing, as it reminds viewers of his long absence from the outside world and the extent of the cultural gap he must bridge. This comedic element underscores Dwight's adaptability and willingness to learn, making him a more relatable character while providing much-needed moments of levity between intense scenes.

Furthermore, Dwight's interactions with the local community provide ample opportunity for humor. His attempts to assert authority in a city that's unaccustomed to organized crime often lead to situations where his hardened demeanor clashes with the laid-back attitudes of Tulsa residents. These interactions highlight Dwight's adaptability and resilience, showing that he's willing to adjust his approach while remaining true to his core principles. The humor derived from these moments not only lightens the narrative but also serves as a tool for character development, allowing viewers to see Dwight's softer, more human side.

Key Moments of Action-Humor Balance

Some of the most memorable moments in *Tulsa King* occur when the show successfully combines action with humor, creating scenes that are thrilling yet tinged with an ironic sense of comedy. One such example is Dwight's early encounter with a group of locals who underestimate his capabilities. In this scene, Dwight is faced with a group of younger, overconfident rivals who assume they can intimidate him due to his age and unfamiliarity with Tulsa. However, Dwight quickly proves otherwise, dispatching his opponents with a mixture of precision and restraint. As the scene unfolds, viewers witness a blend of suspense and humor—the tension of a physical confrontation tempered by the comical realization of the locals that Dwight is far more dangerous than he appears.

Another classic example is Dwight's interactions with technology, particularly his first experience with a smartphone. The humor in these scenes comes not just from his struggles to operate the device but from the contrast between Dwight's old-school persona and the tech-savvy world he now inhabits. This comedic thread continues throughout the series, as Dwight's relationship with technology reflects his larger struggle to adapt to a rapidly changing world. His frustration with digital conveniences adds a humorous, relatable layer to his character, humanizing him and showing that even a mafia capo has his limitations.

These scenes exemplify how *Tulsa King* uses humor to defuse tension and endear Dwight to the audience. The humor never undermines the seriousness of the action but instead enhances it, allowing viewers to connect with Dwight on a deeper level. By blending humor with action, the show creates a rhythm that keeps viewers engaged, alternating between suspenseful sequences and moments of laughter that provide emotional relief.

Supporting Characters as Sources of Humor

The supporting cast in *Tulsa King* also plays a crucial role in balancing action and humor, with each character bringing a unique comedic dynamic to the show. Bodhi, the local bar owner, is one such character. His cautious nature and dry wit often clash with Dwight's bold, no-nonsense approach, creating moments of humor that arise naturally from their interactions. Bodhi's skepticism about Dwight's plans and his reluctance to dive into the criminal underworld serve as humorous counterpoints to Dwight's confidence, highlighting the cultural and personality differences between them.

Another source of humor comes from Tina, the young dealer who represents a new generation of criminals less attached to the traditional rules and codes of the mafia world. Her independent streak and occasional resistance to Dwight's authority create moments of tension that often resolve in humorous exchanges. Dwight's efforts to mentor her are met with varying degrees of success, providing a humorous take on the mentor-mentee dynamic as he tries to pass down "old-school" lessons to someone who operates in a completely different social context.

Mitch, the mechanic, adds humor through his practical, down-to-earth personality. His role as Dwight's logistical support is often marked by his straightforwardness, which contrasts with Dwight's calculated, strategic approach. Mitch's humor is rooted in his simplicity and loyalty, often serving as a foil to Dwight's more complex character. His willingness to support Dwight while poking fun at his grand plans creates a lighthearted dynamic that offsets the tension of their criminal activities.

Action-Humor Synergy: Crafting a Dynamic Viewing Experience

One of the reasons *Tulsa King* excels at blending action and humor is its ability to seamlessly integrate these elements into the story without disrupting the overall tone. Rather than separating action and humor into distinct segments, the show often combines them within the same scene, creating a synergy that keeps viewers on edge while providing moments of levity. This integration allows *Tulsa King* to maintain its pacing and keep the audience engaged, alternating between intensity and humor without detracting from the narrative's progression.

This balance is achieved through meticulous timing and well-crafted dialogue that blends tension with wit. The action sequences are often punctuated by Dwight's dry humor, reflecting his experience and confidence. This synergy allows viewers to feel the stakes of each conflict while remaining entertained by the character's unique perspective on the events unfolding around him. The humor doesn't undercut the action; instead, it enhances it, adding a layer of complexity to the scenes and showcasing Dwight's multifaceted personality.

By blending action and humor so effectively, *Tulsa King* offers a dynamic viewing experience that appeals to a wide audience. The action draws in viewers who appreciate high-stakes drama, while the humor adds a layer of accessibility that makes the story more relatable and enjoyable. This combination also allows the show to explore deeper themes—such as adaptation, resilience, and self-reinvention—without becoming overly heavy or self-serious. The humor lightens the narrative, allowing viewers to reflect on the story's themes while still being entertained.

The Impact of Humor on Dwight's Character Arc

The humor in *Tulsa King* isn't just for entertainment—it also plays a crucial role in Dwight's character development. The comedic elements reveal Dwight's adaptability and resilience, showing that he can laugh at himself and find humor in challenging situations. This sense of humor makes Dwight more approachable, showing that beneath his tough exterior lies a man who is capable of introspection and personal growth. The humor underscores his humanity, allowing viewers to see Dwight not just as a mob boss but as a person trying to navigate an unfamiliar world with grace and flexibility.

Through humor, Dwight's character arc becomes more nuanced, reflecting his journey from a hardened New York capo to a man who learns to embrace new experiences and perspectives. The humor shows Dwight's willingness to adapt and change, even as he holds onto the core principles that define him. This adaptability makes him a compelling protagonist, someone who can both intimidate and amuse, creating a complex, layered character that viewers can root for.

Conclusion: A Perfect Blend for Captivating Storytelling

Tulsa King achieves a remarkable balance between action and humor, creating a viewing experience that is both thrilling and emotionally resonant. The action scenes provide intensity and drive the narrative forward, while the humor adds levity and depth, making the characters more relatable and the storyline more engaging. This blend of action and humor is a testament to the show's craftsmanship, as it maintains a tone that feels authentic and cohesive, despite the contrasting elements.

The combination of action and humor not only entertains but also enhances Dwight's journey, allowing viewers to see different facets of his character and creating a story that resonates on multiple levels. By blending these elements, *Tulsa King* crafts a narrative that is both suspenseful and heartwarming, capturing the essence of a man reinventing himself in a world that challenges everything he knows. Through this unique storytelling approach, *Tulsa King* offers a dynamic and unforgettable experience, showcasing the resilience, adaptability, and enduring humor of Dwight Manfredi.

Chapter 8: The Mafia in a Small Town Setting
Introduction: The Unlikely Backdrop for a Mob Story

The mafia genre has long been associated with sprawling metropolises—cities like New York, Chicago, and Las Vegas serve as natural backdrops for tales of organized crime, where the bustling streets and shadowy alleys offer cover for the underworld's intricate operations. In these urban centers, organized crime is woven into the fabric of the city's life, with connections reaching from the highest echelons of wealth and power down to the gritty street level. *Tulsa King*, however, flips this classic setting on its head by placing Dwight "The General" Manfredi in a small, unassuming town far removed from the familiar structures of organized crime. Tulsa, Oklahoma, with its slower pace, close-knit community, and distinct regional culture, becomes an unlikely stage for a mafia story—one that offers unique challenges and opportunities for a seasoned mobster like Dwight.

This small-town setting forces both Dwight and viewers to reconsider the dynamics of organized crime. Without the anonymity provided by a big city, Tulsa presents new social and logistical obstacles that demand a different approach to power, influence, and control. Dwight is compelled to adapt his tactics, trading in traditional methods of intimidation and underground networks for a more subtle, relationship-focused strategy that respects the town's unique rhythm. In this chapter, we explore how the small-town atmosphere of Tulsa challenges the established mafia genre conventions, highlighting the contrasts and opportunities it creates for Dwight as he seeks to build his empire in an environment far removed from the criminal landscapes of New York.

The Contrast: Big City Mafia vs. Small-Town Dynamics

In the classic mafia narrative, big cities provide the perfect setting for organized crime. These urban landscapes are densely populated and bustling with activity, allowing mobsters to blend into the crowd, conduct business discreetly, and maintain a level of anonymity that is nearly impossible in smaller towns. The sheer size of a city like New York enables different criminal organizations to coexist and establish territories, each with its own hierarchy, rules, and hidden connections to law enforcement and local businesses. The complexity of big-city life mirrors the complexity of the mafia's operations, with each neighborhood or borough operating as part of a larger, interconnected criminal network.

In Tulsa, however, the dynamics are entirely different. The city's smaller population and tightly knit community make it difficult for Dwight to maintain the level of secrecy that organized crime typically demands. The residents are likely to notice a new face in town, especially one as imposing as Dwight's, and rumors spread quickly in a community where people are familiar with one another. Tulsa lacks the layered anonymity of a big city, meaning that Dwight's every move is potentially under scrutiny. This shift forces Dwight to adopt a more restrained and cautious approach, blending in not as an elusive mob boss but as a local businessman with a vested interest in the community.

Additionally, the absence of entrenched crime networks in Tulsa presents both a challenge and an opportunity for Dwight. Unlike New York, where the mafia's infrastructure is already in place, Tulsa requires him to start from scratch, recruiting allies and building connections without the benefit of a preexisting criminal network. While this forces Dwight to work harder to establish his empire, it also grants him a unique level of freedom. With no competing mafia families or heavily policed territories, Tulsa is a blank slate, offering Dwight a chance to build a new kind of power structure—one that blends small-town values with his own criminal expertise.

Adapting Mafia Tactics to a Small Town

The small-town setting of Tulsa requires Dwight to adapt his traditional mafia tactics to fit a new cultural and social environment. In New York, Dwight could rely on intimidation and loyalty-driven fear to maintain control, using violence as a last resort to enforce compliance. However, these tactics are less effective in Tulsa, where the residents are not accustomed to organized crime and are more likely to respond to trust and familiarity than fear. Dwight quickly realizes that if he wants to establish influence, he must earn the respect of the community rather than simply impose his will on it.

One way Dwight adapts is by adopting a quieter, more personable approach. Instead of demanding allegiance, he invests time in getting to know key figures within the community, understanding their needs and priorities. Dwight's charm and charisma come into play here, as he positions himself as a helpful and generous businessman rather than a domineering mob boss. He becomes involved in local affairs, offering support to small businesses and community initiatives, which helps him blend into the town's social fabric. This approach not only earns him the trust of the locals but also grants him a degree of protection, as people are less likely to report his activities if they see him as a positive influence.

Furthermore, Dwight's understanding of small-town values influences his approach to loyalty. In New York, loyalty was often transactional—driven by mutual gain or enforced through fear. But in Tulsa, Dwight learns that loyalty is more personal, based on trust and a sense of belonging. He builds relationships with his allies by treating them as equals, showing a level of respect and reliability that resonates with the town's communal spirit. This shift in tactics allows Dwight to cultivate a loyal network that feels genuinely invested in his success, creating a support base rooted in mutual respect rather than obligation.

The Challenge of Limited Resources and Infrastructure

In the big city, Dwight would have access to a range of resources—money laundering fronts, connections in law enforcement, and an array of criminal experts who could handle specific aspects of his operation. Tulsa, by contrast, lacks these sophisticated resources. The limited infrastructure means that Dwight must be resourceful, working with what's available rather than relying on established systems. His journey in Tulsa is marked by a series of compromises and innovations, as he finds creative solutions to compensate for the lack of big-city resources.

For example, Dwight must establish his own methods for laundering money without the benefit of established financial networks that typically support organized crime. His solution is to work with local businesses, discreetly funneling money through small operations that have minimal oversight. This approach requires a level of discretion and ingenuity, as he must avoid raising suspicion in a community where financial irregularities are more likely to stand out. This forced improvisation adds an element of complexity to his operation, showcasing Dwight's ability to think on his feet and adapt to limited resources.

Moreover, Dwight's access to manpower is limited in Tulsa. In a big city, he could easily recruit muscle from the ranks of underemployed youth or individuals already involved in the underworld. In Tulsa, however, suitable recruits are harder to find, meaning that Dwight must cultivate loyalty and train individuals from the ground up. This scarcity forces Dwight to invest more time and effort into building relationships and instilling loyalty in his recruits, making his organization more cohesive but also more vulnerable to disruptions. The limited manpower challenges Dwight to be strategic, avoiding unnecessary conflict and focusing on maintaining control through influence rather than brute force.

Community Ties and the Challenge of Blending In

In New York, Dwight operated in a world where anonymity was both a shield and a weapon. The vastness of the city allowed him to conduct business without concern for community ties or personal relationships. In Tulsa, however, the close-knit nature of the community means that every action Dwight takes has social repercussions. People talk, rumors spread quickly, and maintaining a low profile is nearly impossible. This lack of anonymity means that Dwight must carefully manage his relationships, balancing his need for influence with the understanding that any misstep could turn the community against him.

To navigate this challenge, Dwight takes a more visible role in Tulsa's social landscape, attending local events, supporting neighborhood initiatives, and making connections with residents who have influence. This visibility is strategic—by positioning himself as an active, invested member of the community, Dwight creates a protective buffer against suspicion. When people see him as a local benefactor rather than a mob boss, they are less likely to question his actions or report his activities to the authorities.

However, blending in also presents unique challenges for Dwight, as he must suppress his natural inclination toward dominance and control. In a big city, he could impose his will without concern for personal relationships, but in Tulsa, he must navigate a web of community ties that require patience, subtlety, and compromise. This tension between his instincts and the demands of the small-town setting adds depth to his character, revealing a man who is willing to adjust his tactics without abandoning his core values.

Law Enforcement in a Small Town: The Tightrope of Influence

In New York, the mafia has a long history of working with law enforcement, using bribery, blackmail, and intimidation to secure protection and maintain operational freedom. In Tulsa, however, Dwight faces a different landscape. Local law enforcement is more familiar with the community and is likely to scrutinize any newcomer who stirs up trouble. With a smaller police force and a more concentrated focus on the town's residents, Dwight cannot rely on the same tactics that worked in New York. Instead, he must build relationships with local officers subtly, avoiding overt bribery or intimidation and instead focusing on creating an understanding based on mutual respect.

One of Dwight's key strategies is to present himself as a stabilizing force in the community, suggesting that his presence could reduce petty crime and keep more volatile criminal elements at bay. By positioning himself as a lesser evil, he builds a rapport with officers who might otherwise be quick to target him. This careful tightrope walk allows Dwight to operate without directly clashing with law enforcement, maintaining a level of autonomy that is essential for his business.

The challenge of dealing with local law enforcement adds an extra layer of tension to Dwight's journey. Unlike New York, where organized crime has a longstanding influence over police departments, Tulsa's law enforcement is less corruptible, more personal, and less inclined to look the other way. This limitation forces Dwight to rely on careful diplomacy and to cultivate alliances with individuals rather than institutions. Through these interactions, we see a more tactical side of Dwight, as he carefully manages relationships with those who hold the power to either protect or dismantle his empire.

The Benefits of Operating in a Small Town

While Tulsa presents unique challenges, it also offers advantages that Dwight is quick to exploit. Without the competitive landscape of a big city, he faces minimal opposition from established crime networks, giving him the freedom to build his operation without interference from rival gangs or syndicates. This lack of competition allows Dwight to create his own power structure, defining the rules and setting the tone for Tulsa's underworld. In this sense, Tulsa becomes a blank canvas, enabling Dwight to implement a vision for organized crime that is uniquely his.

Additionally, the slower pace of small-town life gives Dwight more control over his operations. Unlike the frantic pace of New York, where business must be conducted quickly to avoid detection, Tulsa's unhurried atmosphere allows Dwight to take a measured, strategic approach. He has the time and space to carefully plan each move, building his network with patience and precision. This slower pace also means that law enforcement is less prepared for the kind of criminal organization Dwight is building, allowing him to operate with relative freedom as long as he remains discreet.

The small-town setting also provides Dwight with a level of influence that would be harder to achieve in a big city. By investing in local businesses, supporting community events, and building personal relationships, Dwight gains a reputation that extends beyond his criminal activities. People come to see him as a part of the community, a man who contributes to Tulsa's welfare even as he operates outside the law. This blend of respectability and fear gives Dwight a unique form of power, allowing him to operate without relying solely on intimidation.

Conclusion: Reinventing the Mafia in Tulsa

By setting *Tulsa King* in a small town, the show reinvents the mafia genre, presenting a fresh take on the classic story of power, loyalty, and influence. Tulsa's close-knit community, limited resources, and unique social dynamics force Dwight to adapt, trading in traditional mafia tactics for a more nuanced approach that values relationships, patience, and diplomacy. The small-town setting challenges Dwight to rethink his approach to power, transforming him from a feared New York capo into a community-minded leader who must balance his criminal activities with the expectations and values of Tulsa's residents.

This setting not only creates a unique atmosphere but also provides viewers with a new perspective on organized crime, one that emphasizes adaptability, resilience, and the importance of community ties. Dwight's journey in Tulsa is not just about building an empire; it's about finding a place for himself in a world that is both foreign and familiar, a place where he can redefine what it means to be a leader, a protector, and, ultimately, a mob boss. In Tulsa, Dwight Manfredi becomes more than just "The General"—he becomes a part of the community, blending the traditions of the mafia with the values of small-town life to create a legacy that is as complex and layered as the town itself.

Chapter 9: Dwight's Moral Code
Introduction: The Complex Ethics of a Mafia Man

At first glance, Dwight "The General" Manfredi may appear to be a typical mobster, driven by ambition, power, and a readiness to use violence when necessary. However, beneath the hardened exterior lies a deeply embedded moral code, one shaped by years of loyalty, sacrifice, and personal principles. Dwight's moral compass isn't simplistic or entirely "good," nor does it fit into a conventional ethical framework. Instead, his code of ethics is a complex set of values, forged through years of loyalty to the mafia, tempered by his experience in prison, and continually tested in the new environment of Tulsa.

Dwight's principles influence every action he takes and every relationship he cultivates. Although he operates outside the law, Dwight's decisions are guided by a personal sense of honor, loyalty, and justice. His code is rooted in the mafia's traditional values—respect, loyalty, and an unwavering sense of duty to his chosen family. Yet, his time in prison has also introduced a deeper sense of reflection and pragmatism, leading him to evaluate his past actions and redefine his sense of morality. In this chapter, we'll explore the nuances of Dwight's moral code, examining how it shapes his choices, relationships, and ultimate vision for his life and legacy in *Tulsa King*.

Loyalty Above All: The Foundation of Dwight's Moral Code

One of the cornerstones of Dwight's moral framework is loyalty. For Dwight, loyalty is more than a business transaction; it's a personal commitment that he holds sacred. His loyalty to his mafia family, even after 25 years in prison, exemplifies his dedication to this principle. Unlike many mobsters who view loyalty as a tool for maintaining power, Dwight's loyalty is genuine—he willingly sacrificed his freedom to protect those he served. This dedication to loyalty is rooted in the traditional mafia code, where loyalty is viewed as an unbreakable bond that transcends personal gain or convenience.

In Tulsa, Dwight's loyalty becomes both an asset and a challenge. He expects loyalty from those he trusts, but he also recognizes that it must be earned. Dwight doesn't take loyalty lightly; he's willing to go to great lengths to protect those who stand by him, as long as they reciprocate his commitment. This code shapes his relationships with figures like Bodhi, Mitch, and Tina, whom he sees not merely as allies but as individuals to whom he owes protection and support. However, his loyalty is not blind. When he encounters betrayal or disloyalty, Dwight reacts swiftly and decisively, viewing treachery as an unforgivable offense. His strict adherence to loyalty often puts him in difficult situations, forcing him to balance his principles with the practical needs of his operation.

Dwight's sense of loyalty also extends to his "chosen family" in Tulsa. He views his new allies not simply as business partners but as people he's willing to protect. This sense of loyalty is a double-edged sword, often pulling Dwight into situations where he feels compelled to defend others, even at personal risk. Through this, the show explores how Dwight's loyalty shapes his leadership style and the trust he builds within his network, highlighting his belief that loyalty is a reciprocal relationship based on respect and integrity.

Respect and Honor: The Mafia's Influence on Dwight's Ethics

Respect is another core tenet of Dwight's moral code, rooted deeply in the traditional mafia values that have shaped his life. In Dwight's world, respect is essential—it's the basis for maintaining order, establishing alliances, and securing loyalty. His adherence to respect is evident in how he treats both friends and enemies, always extending a level of courtesy and decorum that is reflective of his old-school approach to power. Dwight believes that respect must be earned, not demanded, and he judges others based on their actions and character rather than their status or title.

Dwight's emphasis on respect also dictates his approach to conflict. He operates with a sense of honor, preferring to resolve disputes diplomatically rather than resorting to unnecessary violence. This restraint doesn't mean Dwight avoids confrontation; rather, he handles it with an air of professionalism, ensuring that his actions are measured and deliberate. He values fair play and expects the same from others, and when he feels disrespected or crossed, he's quick to respond in a way that reasserts his authority without compromising his sense of honor.

In Tulsa, Dwight's commitment to respect often puts him at odds with local figures who lack his sense of decorum. His encounters with figures like Red, the biker gang leader, reveal the clash between Dwight's principles and the more chaotic approach of local criminals. Unlike Dwight, who operates by a strict code, Red is willing to cross lines that Dwight finds unacceptable, leading to a dynamic where Dwight's respect-based philosophy stands in stark contrast to the often disrespectful and unregulated tactics of Tulsa's criminal landscape. This adherence to respect and honor elevates Dwight above the typical thug stereotype, showing him as a man who brings structure, dignity, and a sense of fairness to his dealings.

Violence as a Last Resort: The Controlled Use of Force

Although Dwight is fully capable of violence, he views it as a last resort, a tool to be used only when other options have been exhausted. Unlike impulsive or hot-headed characters, Dwight doesn't relish violence; he sees it as a necessary but regrettable part of his work. This principle is reflective of his pragmatic nature and his belief that violence, when misused, often creates more problems than it solves. His experiences in New York and his time in prison have taught him the importance of restraint and the power of calculated action, values that he brings to his new life in Tulsa.

Dwight's selective use of force is a key component of his moral code. He understands that violence can be an effective tool for maintaining control, but he also knows that it must be wielded carefully. In Tulsa, he uses his reputation and presence to intimidate rather than resorting to immediate aggression, reserving physical confrontation for situations where there's no other recourse. This approach allows Dwight to maintain a level of respect within the community, as people come to see him not as a ruthless tyrant but as a leader who exercises power responsibly.

This restraint is tested as Dwight encounters individuals who operate with far less discipline. Figures like Armand, the local enforcer, often take a more heavy-handed approach, seeing violence as a shortcut to power. Dwight's moral code is tested in these situations, as he must assert his authority while remaining true to his principles. When Dwight does resort to violence, it's a deliberate choice, an assertion of control rather than a display of brutality. Through these moments, *Tulsa King* illustrates how Dwight's ethical code influences his decisions, showing that while he's not afraid to get his hands dirty, he does so with a sense of purpose and responsibility.

Justice and Fairness: A Criminal's Code of Ethics

While Dwight's actions may often place him outside the law, he possesses a deeply ingrained sense of justice and fairness. His idea of justice doesn't align with societal norms or legal standards; instead, it's a personal philosophy rooted in his experiences and the mafia's code. Dwight believes in balancing the scales—repaying loyalty with protection, meeting disrespect with retribution, and honoring agreements to the letter. This sense of justice shapes his interactions with those around him, as he strives to create a world where people can rely on his word and trust in his integrity.

In Tulsa, Dwight's sense of justice plays a significant role in how he builds his criminal empire. Unlike other crime figures who operate solely for profit, Dwight sees himself as a kind of protector, ensuring that those who work with him are treated fairly. This approach attracts individuals who value loyalty and reliability, creating a network of allies who see Dwight as someone they can trust. His fairness also extends to his enemies; while he has little tolerance for betrayal, he respects individuals who act with honor and holds them to the same standard he sets for himself. This sense of justice creates a sense of order within Dwight's operation, giving his empire a structure that differentiates it from the chaos and unpredictability of typical criminal organizations.

Dwight's commitment to justice is tested in his interactions with local figures who lack his ethical grounding. He's often forced to deal with characters who operate solely out of self-interest, lacking any sense of loyalty or respect. These encounters force Dwight to grapple with his own principles, as he must determine how to uphold his sense of justice in a world that doesn't always play by the same rules. Through these challenges, *Tulsa King* delves into the complexities of Dwight's moral code, showing that while he may be a criminal, his actions are guided by a personal sense of ethics that sets him apart.

Mentorship and Responsibility: Dwight as a Leader

As Dwight builds his empire in Tulsa, his role as a mentor and leader becomes an extension of his moral code. He views those in his inner circle as more than just employees or allies; they are individuals for whom he feels a sense of responsibility. This protective instinct is rooted in his belief that leadership requires guidance, respect, and a willingness to nurture loyalty through example. Unlike leaders who rule through fear or manipulation, Dwight aims to cultivate a network of loyal followers by treating them with respect and providing them with a sense of purpose.

This sense of mentorship is particularly evident in his relationship with Tina, the young dealer. Although Dwight could easily exert control over her operation, he chooses to guide her, sharing his wisdom and offering advice rather than enforcing rigid authority. Through his mentorship, Dwight demonstrates his belief in responsibility as a leader, showing that true loyalty comes not from domination but from mutual respect and understanding. His approach to leadership is rooted in empowerment, as he encourages his allies to take ownership of their roles and contribute to the success of his empire.

Dwight's sense of responsibility extends to those outside his immediate circle as well. His interactions with Tulsa's residents reveal a man who genuinely cares about the well-being of the community, even as he operates outside the law. By supporting local businesses, helping struggling individuals, and maintaining a presence in the town, Dwight fosters a sense of unity that benefits both his empire and the community. This approach reinforces his moral code, as he balances his ambition with a sense of duty, ensuring that his actions contribute to the stability and prosperity of those around him.

Integrity and Self-Reflection: A Changed Man

Dwight's moral code is not static; it evolves as he navigates the complexities of his new life in Tulsa. Years in prison forced him to confront the consequences of his actions and reflect on his past, leading to a deeper sense of self-awareness and an understanding of the importance of integrity. This introspection adds layers to Dwight's character, as he strives to build an empire that aligns with his principles and avoids the pitfalls of his former life. He is a man who has learned from his mistakes and is determined to build a legacy that reflects his values.

Throughout the series, Dwight's moments of self-reflection reveal his internal struggle to balance his criminal past with his desire for redemption. He's not blind to the harm his actions can cause, and he wrestles with the ethical implications of his choices. This internal conflict shapes his approach to power, as he strives to create an operation that respects the community and operates with integrity. Dwight's self-awareness also influences his decisions, as he carefully considers the long-term impact of his actions on those he cares about. This focus on integrity demonstrates Dwight's growth, showing that while he may be a mobster, he's also a man striving to live by a code of ethics that transcends the criminal underworld.

Conclusion: A Mobster with a Conscience

Dwight Manfredi's moral code is a complex and evolving set of principles that defines his journey in *Tulsa King*. Rooted in loyalty, respect, justice, and a deep sense of responsibility, Dwight's ethics set him apart from the typical crime figure. While he operates outside the law, his actions are guided by a personal sense of honor and integrity that shapes his relationships, decisions, and leadership style. His code is neither entirely good nor wholly corrupt; it's a nuanced framework that reflects his experiences, his regrets, and his desire to create something lasting.

By exploring Dwight's moral code, *Tulsa King* offers a unique perspective on organized crime, one that challenges conventional depictions of the mafia and presents a character who operates with a conscience. Dwight's journey is a testament to the complexities of morality, showing that even in the darkest of worlds, principles can endure. His actions are guided by a code that values loyalty, justice, and respect, revealing a man who is as driven by ethics as he is by ambition. Through Dwight's story, *Tulsa King* invites viewers to question the boundaries of right and wrong, exploring the idea that even in the shadowy realms of crime, there can be honor, loyalty, and a genuine sense of purpose.

Chapter 10: Themes of Redemption and Adaptation
Introduction: A Journey of Self-Reinvention

At its core, *Tulsa King* is a story of reinvention, following Dwight "The General" Manfredi as he attempts to rebuild his life after decades behind bars. In his journey from a high-ranking New York mafia capo to a man exiled to the quiet town of Tulsa, Dwight finds himself at a crossroads. He must navigate the complexities of a modern world that has left him behind while grappling with the weight of his past actions and searching for redemption in the most unlikely of places. These themes of redemption and adaptation are intricately woven into the fabric of the show, serving as the foundation of Dwight's character arc and providing the driving force behind his actions.

Dwight's journey is more than a quest for power or influence; it's a struggle to reconcile who he was with who he wants to become. For a man shaped by violence, loyalty, and rigid codes of conduct, adapting to a new environment presents both external and internal challenges. In this chapter, we'll explore how *Tulsa King* delves into the themes of redemption and adaptation, examining Dwight's efforts to rebuild his life, make amends for his past, and find a place for himself in a world that has moved forward without him.

Redemption Through Reinvention: Leaving the Past Behind

For Dwight, redemption isn't about erasing his criminal past; it's about finding a way to rebuild his life in a manner that aligns with his values while avoiding the mistakes that led him to prison. After serving 25 years for his loyalty to the mafia, Dwight emerges as a man scarred by his past yet determined to make something meaningful out of his future. His exile to Tulsa becomes an opportunity to start fresh, to create a legacy untainted by the betrayal and violence that defined his former life. This drive for redemption is evident in his every action, as he carefully considers how to build a new empire that reflects his principles without repeating the cycles of harm that he once perpetuated.

Dwight's pursuit of redemption is subtle but constant. He's aware of the lives he has affected and the pain he has caused, and he recognizes that redemption cannot come through a single act. Instead, it's a continuous process that requires him to confront the consequences of his past and strive to be a better person in the present. This journey for self-reinvention is reflected in his approach to Tulsa's criminal landscape. Rather than replicating the ruthless tactics he used in New York, Dwight adopts a more ethical approach, emphasizing loyalty, fairness, and respect. Through his actions, he aims to create a network that is less about brute power and more about mutual benefit, offering protection and stability to those who work with him rather than fear and coercion.

This reinvention is as much about Dwight's internal growth as it is about his external success. As he builds his new empire, he's constantly questioning his motives, evaluating his methods, and adjusting his approach to ensure that his actions align with his sense of justice. By reinventing himself in Tulsa, Dwight isn't just seeking to establish control; he's striving to find a way to exist in a world that is both different and, in some ways, kinder than the one he left behind.

Atonement and Responsibility: Making Amends

Dwight's quest for redemption isn't only about his personal growth—it's also about taking responsibility for the people he harmed, directly or indirectly, during his time in the mafia. Though he doesn't often vocalize his regrets, Dwight's actions reveal a desire to atone for his past. He feels a sense of responsibility toward the people in his life, both old and new, and he's willing to go to great lengths to protect and support those who stand by him. This sense of duty becomes a driving force in his relationships, as he seeks to offer stability and guidance to those who join his network in Tulsa.

In particular, Dwight's relationship with Tina, a young dealer he mentors, reflects his desire for atonement. Though he's not trying to undo his past mistakes, he sees an opportunity to prevent Tina from making similar choices. By offering her guidance and protection, Dwight tries to steer her away from the pitfalls that defined his own life, giving her the chance to build a future free from the constraints of organized crime. This relationship is both a form of mentorship and an act of redemption, allowing Dwight to indirectly make amends for the harm he has caused by helping others avoid the same fate.

Dwight's sense of responsibility also extends to the broader community of Tulsa. Unlike his life in New York, where his influence was confined to the criminal underworld, Dwight actively involves himself in the welfare of Tulsa's residents, supporting local businesses, attending community events, and offering assistance to those in need. By integrating himself into the community, Dwight isn't just seeking acceptance; he's seeking forgiveness, hoping that his positive contributions will outweigh the harm he once caused. Through his actions, Dwight tries to build a legacy that goes beyond crime, one that reflects a commitment to making the world around him a little better than he found it.

Confronting Change: The Challenge of Adapting to the Modern World

For Dwight, adapting to the modern world is both a practical challenge and a symbolic one. His 25 years in prison have left him disconnected from technology, social norms, and the cultural shifts that have reshaped society in his absence. This disconnect is evident in his initial struggles with smartphones, social media, and other aspects of modern life, which often become sources of both frustration and humor. These moments of adaptation highlight the vast cultural gap Dwight must bridge, illustrating the difficulties of reentering a world that has evolved without him.

Yet, Dwight's adaptation goes beyond learning how to use a smartphone or navigate social media. He must also adjust his mindset, recognizing that the rigid rules and unspoken codes that once governed his life no longer hold the same weight. The world has become more complex, and people are less willing to accept authoritarian leadership or coercion. This shift challenges Dwight to rethink his approach to power, forcing him to adopt a more flexible, open-minded perspective that values cooperation and mutual benefit over control.

Dwight's adaptation is particularly evident in his approach to leadership. Unlike the mafia hierarchy of New York, where loyalty was often enforced through fear, Tulsa requires a different approach. Dwight learns to value dialogue, compromise, and respect, building relationships based on trust rather than intimidation. This process of adaptation is a test of his character, revealing his willingness to grow and change in response to new circumstances. Through this journey, Dwight not only learns to navigate the modern world but also develops a new understanding of what it means to lead, creating a dynamic that reflects both his old-school values and his evolving perspective.

Finding Purpose in Exile: From Power to Meaning

Dwight's exile to Tulsa represents both a punishment and an opportunity for self-discovery. Stripped of his former life, status, and connections, he's forced to confront the question of what truly matters to him. In New York, power and loyalty were his guiding principles, but in Tulsa, he begins to explore the possibility of finding a deeper sense of purpose. His decision to establish a new network isn't just about building an empire; it's about creating something meaningful, something that reflects his personal values rather than the expectations of others.

In Tulsa, Dwight's motivations begin to shift from accumulating power to leaving a legacy that he can be proud of. He becomes more invested in the well-being of his allies, viewing them not as assets but as individuals who deserve respect and support. His desire to make a positive impact extends beyond his own ambitions, as he starts to see himself as a protector, a mentor, and even a father figure to those who rely on him. This evolution in purpose is a key aspect of Dwight's redemption, as he moves away from the selfish pursuits of his past and focuses on creating a community that aligns with his sense of justice and honor.

Through this journey, *Tulsa King* explores the idea that redemption is not a single act but a lifelong pursuit. Dwight's search for purpose is a form of redemption in itself, allowing him to redefine his life on his own terms. He is no longer bound by the expectations of the mafia; he's free to create a legacy that reflects his personal values, offering him a chance to make amends not only to others but to himself.

Embracing Vulnerability and Self-Reflection

One of the most significant aspects of Dwight's journey is his willingness to confront his own vulnerability. In his past life, Dwight was known for his strength, resilience, and unwavering loyalty, qualities that allowed him to survive in the ruthless world of organized crime. But in Tulsa, he begins to explore parts of himself that he once buried, opening up to self-reflection and acknowledging the emotional scars left by his years in prison and his life in the mafia. This willingness to embrace vulnerability is a testament to Dwight's growth, showing that he's no longer defined solely by his toughness or his status.

Dwight's moments of self-reflection reveal a man who is haunted by his past yet determined to find peace in his present. He's aware of the choices he made, the lives he affected, and the personal cost of his loyalty to the mafia. This self-awareness adds layers to his character, showing that while he may be a criminal, he is also a man searching for redemption. Through his internal struggles, Dwight comes to terms with the complexity of his own identity, acknowledging that redemption isn't about erasing the past but about finding a way to live with it.

This vulnerability also strengthens Dwight's relationships, as it allows him to connect with others on a more personal level. By sharing his experiences and offering guidance, he builds trust with his allies, creating a sense of camaraderie that goes beyond business. This openness humanizes Dwight, making him a character who is not only strong but also compassionate and self-aware. His willingness to confront his own flaws and make amends adds depth to his journey, allowing him to move forward without denying the person he once was.

Redemption Through Community: Building Something Lasting

In Tulsa, Dwight's pursuit of redemption takes on a communal dimension. Unlike his life in New York, where his actions were confined to the criminal underworld, his presence in Tulsa impacts the entire community. By investing in local businesses, supporting neighborhood initiatives, and forging relationships with residents, Dwight begins to build a network that goes beyond crime. He becomes a part of the community, contributing to its stability and growth while maintaining a level of respectability that benefits both his empire and the town.

This sense of community is a significant aspect of Dwight's redemption. For a man who once operated in the shadows, becoming a visible and respected figure in Tulsa offers a new form of fulfillment. He's no longer just a mob boss; he's a mentor, a benefactor, and a leader who cares about the people around him. This communal focus adds depth to Dwight's journey, as he realizes that redemption isn't just about personal growth—it's about leaving a positive impact on the world. Through his actions, Dwight transforms Tulsa into a place of second chances, not only for himself but for those who choose to follow him.

In building a community based on respect, loyalty, and mutual benefit, Dwight creates a legacy that reflects his values. This focus on community allows him to achieve a form of redemption that is rooted in action rather than words, proving that he's capable of creating something meaningful despite his past. Through his journey in Tulsa, Dwight finds a sense of belonging that he never experienced in New York, allowing him to redefine what it means to be part of something larger than himself.

Conclusion: A Journey of Redemption and Adaptation

In *Tulsa King*, the themes of redemption and adaptation are intricately connected, reflecting Dwight Manfredi's complex journey as he rebuilds his life after prison. His quest for redemption is not about erasing his past or abandoning his principles; it's about finding a way to live with his choices, make amends, and create a future that reflects his values. Through his adaptation to the modern world and his integration into the Tulsa community, Dwight discovers that redemption is a continuous process, one that requires self-reflection, responsibility, and a commitment to positive change.

Dwight's journey is a testament to the resilience of the human spirit, showing that even in the face of exile, loss, and regret, it's possible to find meaning and purpose. His adaptation to Tulsa's unique culture challenges him to rethink his approach to power, loyalty, and community, allowing him to reinvent himself without abandoning his core principles. Through this process, Dwight's search for redemption becomes not only a personal journey but a transformative experience for the community he builds around him.

In *Tulsa King*, redemption is portrayed as a dynamic, evolving journey, one that requires Dwight to confront his past while embracing his future. Through his efforts to adapt, rebuild, and make amends, Dwight embodies the idea that redemption is achievable even in the unlikeliest of places, proving that true change comes not from escaping one's past but from finding a way to live with it in a way that brings peace, purpose, and, ultimately, forgiveness.

Chapter 11: The Criminal Underworld of Tulsa
Introduction: Building a Criminal Empire in a Small Town

Unlike the bustling, densely populated cities of traditional mafia tales, Tulsa presents an unfamiliar and sparse landscape for organized crime. This setting requires Dwight "The General" Manfredi to navigate a different kind of underworld, one that lacks the established networks and longstanding rivalries of New York. While Tulsa may not have the entrenched crime syndicates of larger cities, it does host its own fragmented network of local criminals, independent operators, and small-time gangs. These factions operate in silos, each with its unique turf and influence, and all of them view Dwight's arrival with a mixture of curiosity, suspicion, and hostility.

Dwight's interactions with Tulsa's criminal factions reveal both his adaptability and strategic prowess. Unlike his life in New York, where power was asserted through loyalty-driven fear and well-established hierarchies, Tulsa's underworld requires him to take a more diplomatic, calculated approach. He must understand the dynamics, personalities, and motivations of the players within this decentralized network, as well as navigate an often unpredictable relationship with local law enforcement. This chapter explores the various factions within Tulsa's criminal underworld, detailing Dwight's interactions with them and examining how he manages these relationships to build his own empire in a city unaccustomed to his brand of organized crime.

The Landscape of Crime in Tulsa: Fragmented and Independent

Unlike the streamlined structure of New York's mafia families, Tulsa's criminal underworld is fragmented, populated by small, independent factions that often operate with little coordination or oversight. Rather than mafia-style hierarchies, Tulsa's criminals are mostly independent operators—dealers, biker gangs, smugglers, and low-level enforcers—each pursuing profit with minimal allegiance to a greater criminal organization. This loose network allows for individual autonomy, making it difficult for any single player to control or influence the entire underworld. In this disjointed environment, Dwight quickly recognizes that establishing power will require careful alliances, as he cannot rely on a unified network to support his rise.

The fragmented nature of Tulsa's criminal underworld is both a challenge and an opportunity for Dwight. While it means there is no central power to dethrone, it also requires him to navigate a web of disparate players, each with its turf, reputation, and sometimes unpredictable responses. For Dwight, the absence of a structured criminal hierarchy in Tulsa means he must build his power base from scratch, forging alliances with small-time operators and building a network of loyalists who will support his vision. To succeed, he must transform this loose network into a cohesive operation, one that functions with the precision and loyalty of the mafia families he once served.

The Local Factions: Key Players in Tulsa's Underworld

Tulsa's criminal underworld consists of various independent factions, each with its territory, rules, and goals. These key players form the foundation of Tulsa's crime landscape, and Dwight's interactions with them shape his approach to building his empire.

1. The Biker Gang Led by Red

Red and his biker gang represent one of the more prominent factions within Tulsa's criminal landscape. They control a portion of the city's drug and weapons trafficking, leveraging their mobility and street presence to maintain a grip on local crime. Unlike Dwight, who operates with a sense of honor and strategy, Red's gang uses brute force, relying on intimidation and violence to control their territory. Red's leadership style is aggressive, making him a natural rival to Dwight, whose arrival threatens to disrupt the gang's operations and influence.

From their first encounter, Red perceives Dwight as a threat. Used to operating without interference, he views Dwight's presence as an intrusion into his territory and reacts with hostility. Dwight, however, approaches Red with a mix of caution and assertiveness, recognizing that an outright conflict could draw unnecessary attention from law enforcement. Instead, Dwight uses his reputation and presence to assert control, demonstrating to Red that he's not intimidated and that he has no intention of backing down. Through a series of strategic moves, Dwight gradually earns a grudging respect from Red, who comes to realize that Dwight is not just another small-time player but a force capable of reshaping Tulsa's criminal landscape.

Red's gang serves as both a challenge and a foil for Dwight. Their presence underscores the difference between Dwight's strategic approach and the more chaotic methods of local criminals. Over time, Dwight finds ways to work around the gang's influence, either by negotiating territory agreements or by using his own network to counter their influence. Red's gang becomes an ongoing obstacle, forcing Dwight to continuously prove his strength and adaptability in the face of a powerful rival faction.

2. The Small-Time Dealers and Street-Level Operators

In addition to Red's gang, Tulsa's criminal landscape includes numerous small-time dealers and street-level operators, each working independently to turn a profit. These dealers operate in specific neighborhoods, catering to local customers without attempting to expand beyond their small territories. While they lack the resources and manpower of Red's gang, they represent an important part of Tulsa's drug trade, as they control access to local buyers and have established relationships within the community.

Dwight's interactions with these operators are marked by a mixture of respect and pragmatism. Unlike Red, who sees him as a direct competitor, these small-time dealers view Dwight as an outsider who could offer resources and protection. Recognizing the potential for mutual benefit, Dwight approaches them with a collaborative mindset, offering them access to his supply chain and protection in exchange for loyalty and a cut of the profits. This approach allows Dwight to gradually incorporate them into his network, creating a decentralized distribution network that strengthens his reach within Tulsa.

Through these partnerships, Dwight gains access to new markets while also providing small-time dealers with a level of security they didn't previously have. His willingness to work with independent operators reflects his adaptability, as he recognizes that outright control is less effective in a community where trust and local reputation are valued. This decentralized approach allows him to build influence gradually, creating a network that feels less like a traditional criminal hierarchy and more like a cooperative enterprise.

3. The Mechanic Network: Mitch and His Role in Logistics

Mitch, a mechanic with a sideline in stolen car parts, plays a unique role in Dwight's operation, serving as the logistical backbone of his network. Mitch's knowledge of transportation and his ability to move products discreetly make him invaluable, especially in a city where transportation is essential for distributing goods without attracting law enforcement attention. Through Mitch, Dwight is able to build a reliable supply chain, using the mechanic's contacts and resources to transport goods across the city.

Dwight's relationship with Mitch goes beyond a simple business partnership; it's built on mutual trust and respect. Unlike other players in Tulsa's underworld, Mitch views Dwight as a mentor, someone who brings experience and guidance to an often chaotic environment. In return, Mitch offers loyalty and logistical expertise, helping Dwight manage the complexities of distribution without drawing attention. This alliance highlights Dwight's ability to cultivate loyalty by treating his allies with respect, creating a network of individuals who are invested in his success.

Through Mitch, Dwight gains access to a network of transporters and logistics experts, allowing him to expand his operation without relying on the traditional channels of organized crime. This decentralized logistics network gives Dwight a significant advantage, as it allows him to move goods discreetly and maintain control over his distribution channels. Mitch's role exemplifies Dwight's strategic approach, as he builds his empire through alliances that prioritize loyalty and expertise over brute force.

Navigating Law Enforcement: Dwight's Delicate Balance

While Tulsa's criminal factions pose challenges and opportunities for Dwight, his interactions with local law enforcement are a different kind of balancing act. Unlike New York, where the mafia has long-standing influence over police forces, Tulsa's law enforcement is less corruptible, more personal, and more integrated into the community. This difference requires Dwight to adopt a cautious approach, as he knows that any misstep could attract unwanted scrutiny and disrupt his entire operation.

Dwight's relationship with Stacy, a local police officer, is particularly significant. Stacy is initially suspicious of Dwight, viewing him as a potential threat to Tulsa's stability. However, as she observes his actions and recognizes his desire to bring order to Tulsa's chaotic underworld, she develops a begrudging respect for him. Stacy's role as both a protector of the law and a pragmatic figure creates a dynamic in which Dwight must constantly navigate her scrutiny while demonstrating that his presence benefits the community.

Rather than attempting to bribe or intimidate Stacy, Dwight uses diplomacy and discretion, recognizing that her cooperation—or at least her neutrality—will be critical to his long-term success. He approaches her with respect, carefully crafting an unspoken understanding that his actions are meant to stabilize the underworld rather than destabilize the community. This relationship forces Dwight to constantly weigh the risks and rewards of his actions, as he must ensure that his empire remains under the radar while avoiding any direct conflict with law enforcement.

Through his interactions with Stacy and other officers, *Tulsa King* illustrates Dwight's skill at walking the fine line between criminality and respectability. His ability to navigate this delicate balance allows him to build a network that operates with relative freedom, as he cultivates a reputation that positions him as a lesser evil in the eyes of the law. This relationship with law enforcement reflects Dwight's understanding of power and influence, as he recognizes that true control requires both respect and restraint.

Building a New Kind of Criminal Empire: Dwight's Strategic Alliances

Dwight's journey in Tulsa is marked by his ability to forge alliances that reflect his personal code of loyalty, respect, and mutual benefit. Unlike his life in New York, where power was often asserted through fear and coercion, Dwight's approach in Tulsa is more collaborative, focusing on building a network of individuals who share his vision. This approach allows him to create an empire that operates more like a cooperative enterprise than a traditional crime syndicate, with each member contributing to a shared goal of stability, profit, and protection.

Through his alliances with local criminals, small-time operators, and law enforcement, Dwight creates a network that functions as both a criminal empire and a support system. His willingness to work with independent operators and small-time dealers demonstrates his adaptability, as he recognizes that success in Tulsa requires a different approach to power. By incorporating these individuals into his network, Dwight is able to build influence without disrupting the community, creating a network that feels organic and rooted in mutual trust.

This cooperative approach also reflects Dwight's personal growth, as he learns to adapt his methods to suit the unique dynamics of Tulsa. He is no longer driven solely by a desire for control; instead, he seeks to create something lasting and meaningful, a legacy that reflects his values and respects the people who support him. Through this journey, Dwight's empire becomes a reflection of his own evolution, as he builds a network that is less about dominance and more about loyalty, respect, and shared purpose.

Conclusion: The New King of Tulsa's Underworld

In *Tulsa King*, Dwight's interactions with the various factions of Tulsa's criminal underworld reveal both his adaptability and his strategic brilliance. Faced with a fragmented network of small-time criminals, independent operators, and cautious law enforcement, Dwight must navigate a complex web of relationships to establish his power. By forming alliances that prioritize mutual benefit and respect, he transforms Tulsa's underworld from a chaotic landscape into a cohesive network, one that reflects his own values of loyalty, respect, and responsibility.

Through his relationships with Red's biker gang, small-time dealers, Mitch's logistics network, and law enforcement, Dwight builds an empire that is both stable and adaptable, capable of thriving within the unique dynamics of Tulsa. His cooperative approach reflects his personal growth, as he learns to balance ambition with ethics, creating a network that operates with precision and loyalty. This approach not only cements his place as a respected figure in Tulsa's underworld but also creates a lasting legacy, one that embodies his journey of reinvention, redemption, and resilience.

As the new king of Tulsa's criminal underworld, Dwight Manfredi proves that power isn't just about control—it's about influence, integrity, and the ability to inspire loyalty in those who stand beside him. Through his journey, *Tulsa King* offers a fresh perspective on organized crime, showing that even in the shadowy realms of the underworld, principles and respect can shape an empire.

Chapter 12: The Impact of Technology on the Modern Mafia
Introduction: An Old-School Mobster in a Digital World

In *Tulsa King*, Dwight "The General" Manfredi emerges from prison after 25 years to find a world that has changed in ways he could have never imagined. No longer surrounded by the familiar analog systems that governed the mafia's operations in the past, he is thrust into a modern world shaped by digital technology, social media, and advanced surveillance. For a man who once relied on face-to-face meetings, hand-delivered messages, and untraceable landlines, the ubiquity of smartphones, digital payments, and online communication presents both a challenge and an opportunity. These technologies have revolutionized the way criminal enterprises operate, and Dwight must either adapt to these changes or risk becoming obsolete.

Dwight's struggle with technology is more than a humorous subplot; it represents a fundamental shift in the way organized crime is conducted. Technology has redefined every aspect of life, including the underworld, where anonymity and discretion are essential. Dwight's journey is one of adaptation as he learns to navigate the technological landscape, both leveraging it for his empire and contending with its challenges. In this chapter, we'll explore how technology impacts Dwight's operations, influences his interactions with Tulsa's criminal landscape, and underscores the clash between his old-school values and the digital age.

The Challenge of Adapting to Digital Communication

One of the most immediate hurdles Dwight faces upon his release is adapting to the prevalence of digital communication. The days of coded phrases, clandestine meetings, and trusted messengers are gone; now, smartphones, text messages, and social media dominate the way people connect. For Dwight, who values privacy and is cautious about leaving any trace, the transparency and accessibility of digital communication are disconcerting. From his perspective, the idea of discussing business over a phone that can easily be tracked or intercepted is risky, if not reckless.

Dwight's distrust of smartphones and other forms of digital communication reflects his old-school mafia roots. He is accustomed to face-to-face interactions, where he can gauge trustworthiness and control the flow of information. The reliance on digital messaging and calls feels like an invitation for surveillance, and he is initially skeptical about adopting these tools. However, he soon realizes that adapting to this form of communication is essential if he wants to connect with his allies, keep up with his competition, and maintain influence within Tulsa's criminal underworld.

In navigating this digital communication landscape, Dwight is often forced to rely on others who are more tech-savvy. Figures like Bodhi and Tina help bridge the gap, introducing him to basic smartphone functions, text messaging, and even secure messaging apps. This reliance highlights Dwight's adaptability and willingness to learn, showing that he can embrace change despite his initial resistance. Through these moments, *Tulsa King* explores Dwight's struggle to reconcile his desire for control with the need to trust others, a theme that reflects the broader challenges of leadership in a technology-driven world.

Surveillance and Privacy: The Risks of a Digital World

For a seasoned mobster like Dwight, maintaining privacy is crucial. In the past, organized crime relied on face-to-face interactions, secret codes, and untraceable cash transactions to avoid detection. However, the modern world is filled with surveillance cameras, digital records, and government monitoring programs that make it far more difficult to operate discreetly. Dwight's awareness of these risks is evident in his cautious approach to digital communication, as he recognizes that any misstep could expose him to law enforcement or rival factions.

The ubiquity of surveillance cameras in Tulsa presents a particular challenge for Dwight. Unlike New York, where crowded streets and anonymity provided some cover, Tulsa's smaller, tightly-knit community means that Dwight's movements are more noticeable. Surveillance cameras capture his presence in public spaces, limiting his ability to operate freely without leaving a digital trail. This constant visibility forces Dwight to be strategic, carefully planning his movements and using trusted allies to gather information or conduct business in locations less likely to be monitored.

Moreover, Dwight's reluctance to use digital banking or payment apps speaks to his awareness of the risks associated with leaving a financial trail. Cash transactions were once the lifeblood of the mafia, but in today's world, cash is less common, and digital transactions have become the norm. Dwight's adjustment to this new reality is slow; he remains skeptical of using digital payment systems, viewing them as a potential vulnerability that could reveal his activities. His aversion to these modern conveniences highlights his instinctual understanding of security, showing that while technology offers convenience, it also comes with a new set of risks.

The Power of Social Media: Building Reputation in the Digital Age

In the age of social media, reputation is built as much online as it is in person. Unlike the old mafia world, where one's reputation was established through word of mouth, social media platforms now offer a new avenue for visibility and influence. Dwight's initial reaction to social media is one of bewilderment; he struggles to see how these platforms could be relevant to his operations, let alone beneficial. However, he soon realizes that in Tulsa's modern landscape, social media plays a significant role in shaping public perception and building trust within the community.

Through his allies, Dwight begins to understand the value of social media as a tool for branding. Figures like Tina, who have a younger, more connected social network, help him see how social media can be used subtly to build a positive reputation and project a certain image. For instance, local businesses associated with Dwight's network gain traction as his allies post about events, partnerships, and charitable activities online. This digital presence allows Dwight to foster goodwill within the community, positioning himself as a benefactor rather than a traditional mob boss. By adapting his image to suit modern expectations, Dwight learns to leverage social media as an indirect tool for influence, building a reputation that is both respected and discreet.

Social media also offers Dwight insight into his competition. Through careful monitoring, he gains valuable information about rival factions and potential threats, allowing him to stay one step ahead without engaging in direct conflict. This use of social media for intelligence gathering reflects his adaptability, as he recognizes the advantages of embracing digital tools to maintain control over his environment. By integrating social media into his strategy, Dwight demonstrates his ability to navigate the complexities of a world that values online presence as much as personal reputation.

The Influence of Digital Payment Systems on Organized Crime

One of the most significant changes Dwight faces is the impact of digital payment systems on the criminal underworld. Cash transactions, once the standard for avoiding detection, are increasingly rare in the modern world, replaced by digital wallets, apps, and cryptocurrency. These innovations complicate Dwight's operations, as he must find ways to conduct business without leaving a financial trail that could expose his network to scrutiny.

Dwight's reluctance to embrace digital payments initially limits his ability to operate smoothly in Tulsa. Transactions that would have once been handled in cash now require a level of digital literacy, and Dwight is forced to adapt his approach to accommodate this shift. With the help of allies like Mitch, who understands both the practical aspects of logistics and the necessity of discretion, Dwight learns to navigate these systems without compromising his security. He gradually incorporates digital payment methods into his operation, relying on his allies to manage these transactions while maintaining a degree of distance from the technology itself.

Cryptocurrency, in particular, offers Dwight a new avenue for secure transactions, as it provides a level of anonymity that aligns with his need for privacy. Although initially skeptical of the complex and volatile world of digital currency, Dwight learns to use cryptocurrency for certain transactions, reducing the risk of detection. This willingness to experiment with new financial systems demonstrates his adaptability and willingness to learn, as he recognizes that traditional cash transactions alone are no longer sufficient to support his empire. Through these adjustments, *Tulsa King* shows how Dwight's understanding of finance and discretion evolves in response to the digital age, revealing the complexities of managing money in a world that no longer relies solely on physical currency.

Cybersecurity: Protecting Sensitive Information

In the digital world, cybersecurity is paramount, especially for someone operating outside the law. Dwight's initial lack of understanding around cybersecurity poses a significant risk, as he's unfamiliar with the complexities of data protection and encryption. Unlike the analog methods of his past, where sensitive information was guarded through physical secrecy, modern criminals must navigate the digital landscape carefully to protect their networks and communications from hacking, monitoring, and leaks.

Dwight's learning curve is steep. He begins by relying heavily on allies who have a greater understanding of digital security, using their knowledge to implement basic protections for his network. Bodhi, with his awareness of digital risks and experience in the bar business, becomes instrumental in teaching Dwight about the importance of secure communication channels, encrypted messaging apps, and protecting devices from hacking. Over time, Dwight learns to use these tools to secure his operation, though he maintains a healthy skepticism about the technology's vulnerabilities.

Despite his growing familiarity with cybersecurity, Dwight is careful not to become too dependent on digital systems. He recognizes that technology is a double-edged sword—it offers efficiency and reach, but it also increases the risk of exposure. This cautious approach reinforces Dwight's old-school instincts, showing that while he may adapt to new methods, he remains wary of the potential for digital surveillance and betrayal. His understanding of cybersecurity reflects his ability to learn without sacrificing his principles, blending traditional discretion with modern tools to protect his empire.

Technology as a Double-Edged Sword: New Opportunities and New Risks

While modern technology offers Dwight new opportunities to expand his network, gather intelligence, and manage finances, it also comes with inherent risks. Surveillance cameras, smartphones, and digital records mean that every move he makes can be tracked, recorded, and potentially exposed. This visibility is a constant threat, as any digital misstep could bring law enforcement to his doorstep. Dwight's cautious approach reflects his awareness of these risks, showing that he's willing to adapt without becoming complacent.

At the same time, technology provides Dwight with unique advantages. Social media allows him to subtly shape his public image, digital payment systems offer anonymity, and encrypted communication protects his network from prying eyes. This dual nature of technology—the benefits and the dangers—underscores the delicate balance Dwight must maintain as he navigates the digital landscape. He recognizes that while technology can aid his operations, it also requires constant vigilance to avoid exposure.

Through his journey, *Tulsa King* illustrates the impact of technology on the modern mafia, showing that even the most seasoned mobster must adapt to survive in a world where privacy is a luxury and information is power. Dwight's interactions with technology highlight the complexities of criminal enterprise in the digital age, where new tools offer both opportunities and threats. His ability to embrace technology while remaining cautious reflects his adaptability, as he learns to leverage modern tools without compromising his core values.

Conclusion: An Adaptable King in a Digital Kingdom

In *Tulsa King*, Dwight Manfredi's struggle to adapt to modern technology is emblematic of the broader challenges faced by organized crime in the digital age. For Dwight, technology represents both a threat to his privacy and a tool for expanding his influence. His initial resistance gives way to cautious acceptance, as he learns to use digital communication, social media, cybersecurity, and cryptocurrency to his advantage. These technological adjustments highlight his resilience and willingness to evolve, showing that even an old-school mobster can thrive in a world dominated by digital innovation.

Dwight's journey is one of adaptation and growth, as he confronts his distrust of technology and finds ways to incorporate it into his empire without sacrificing his values. His interactions with modern tools reveal a man who is as strategic as he is cautious, balancing the benefits of technology with the need for discretion. By navigating these challenges, Dwight solidifies his place as a leader capable of blending traditional wisdom with modern innovation.

Through Dwight's experiences, *Tulsa King* explores the impact of technology on the modern mafia, illustrating the complexities of operating in a world where every move is traceable and every transaction is recorded. Dwight's ability to adapt reflects his strength as a leader, showing that while the rules may change, the qualities that define true power—intelligence, loyalty, and resilience—remain timeless. In Tulsa, Dwight becomes not only a king of the underworld but a testament to the power of adaptability, proving that even in a world transformed by technology, the old ways still hold value when combined with a willingness to learn.

Chapter 13: Loyalty and Betrayal
Introduction: The Twin Pillars of Loyalty and Betrayal

In *Tulsa King*, loyalty and betrayal are central themes that shape Dwight "The General" Manfredi's journey and define his relationships. For Dwight, loyalty is not just a principle—it's the foundation of his identity. Having dedicated 25 years of his life to the mafia, serving his time in prison without ever betraying those he served, Dwight embodies a level of loyalty that is unwavering and absolute. But his past experiences have also taught him the painful reality that loyalty is a rare and costly commodity, one that is often met with betrayal.

As Dwight builds his new empire in Tulsa, he encounters a cast of characters whose loyalty—or lack thereof—forces him to confront his expectations and adapt his understanding of trust. These experiences become a test of his ability to discern true loyalty from opportunism, while betrayal serves as a constant reminder of the fragile bonds that often govern relationships in the underworld. This chapter explores how loyalty and betrayal influence Dwight's decisions, shape his relationships, and ultimately define his leadership style as he navigates the complex social web of Tulsa's criminal landscape.

Loyalty as a Cornerstone of Dwight's Code

Loyalty is the backbone of Dwight's moral code, a value that defines his every action and decision. In the world Dwight grew up in, loyalty was paramount; it wasn't merely expected but demanded, forming the foundation upon which the mafia operated. His loyalty to the family was tested during his 25-year prison sentence, a punishment he accepted without complaint, choosing silence over betrayal. For Dwight, loyalty isn't transactional—it's a commitment that he holds sacred, regardless of the personal cost.

As Dwight builds his empire in Tulsa, he brings this deep-seated loyalty with him, expecting the same in return from those who work alongside him. However, Tulsa's decentralized and less formal criminal network presents a new challenge. Unlike the mafia, where loyalty was ingrained in the culture, Tulsa's independent operators and small-time criminals are often driven by profit rather than commitment. This lack of a shared loyalty structure forces Dwight to adapt, finding ways to cultivate trust and loyalty in an environment where personal benefit often outweighs allegiance.

Throughout the series, Dwight's dedication to loyalty manifests in his leadership style. He offers protection, guidance, and support to those who align with him, treating them as members of a family rather than mere assets. Dwight's loyalty is a rare quality in Tulsa, where trust is in short supply, and his consistent adherence to this principle earns him the respect and devotion of figures like Bodhi, Mitch, and Tina. By demonstrating loyalty through action, Dwight builds a network of individuals who recognize that he values their loyalty as much as he values their skills, fostering a sense of unity that transcends traditional criminal alliances.

Betrayal as a Painful Reality

Despite his unwavering loyalty, Dwight is no stranger to betrayal. His time in the mafia exposed him to countless instances of betrayal, from minor infractions to outright treachery, leaving him with a hardened view of human nature. His prison sentence itself is a testament to this betrayal; while Dwight remained loyal to the mafia, the family repaid his silence with exile, sending him to Tulsa rather than welcoming him back into the fold. This experience shapes Dwight's understanding of loyalty, making him aware that even the strongest bonds can be severed when convenience or profit is at stake.

In Tulsa, Dwight's understanding of betrayal takes on new dimensions as he encounters individuals whose loyalty is often situational. Figures like Red, the leader of a local biker gang, test Dwight's patience by challenging his authority and occasionally undermining his efforts. Red's allegiance is rooted in self-interest rather than loyalty, and his actions serve as a reminder that betrayal can come from those who don't fully commit to Dwight's vision. Dwight's interactions with Red and other opportunistic figures illustrate his pragmatism; while he values loyalty, he's prepared for betrayal, recognizing that trust must be carefully earned and vigilantly maintained.

Betrayal also comes from unexpected sources, such as local figures who initially pledge their support but waver when faced with risks or personal gains. These moments of betrayal test Dwight's resilience, forcing him to confront the limitations of loyalty in a world where commitment is often conditional. Through these experiences, Dwight learns that betrayal is an inevitable aspect of leadership, one that requires him to constantly evaluate the motives of those around him. His willingness to address betrayal decisively yet pragmatically shows his understanding that while loyalty is valuable, it cannot always be guaranteed.

Old Relationships: Testing Loyalties from Dwight's Past

Dwight's loyalty isn't confined to his new alliances in Tulsa; he carries with him a complex web of relationships from his past, each marked by its own history of loyalty and betrayal. His loyalty to the mafia family he once served is evident in his willingness to sacrifice decades of his life, yet his exile to Tulsa highlights the betrayal he suffered at their hands. This experience shapes Dwight's outlook, making him cautious about forming new alliances and wary of trusting others too quickly. His commitment to loyalty is genuine, but he is no longer naive; he understands that loyalty must be mutual and earned.

Despite his exile, Dwight still holds a sense of loyalty to the people who shaped his past, demonstrating that his commitment to the mafia was not just to the organization but to the individuals he respected. When he encounters old associates or individuals with ties to New York, Dwight's loyalty to his past resurfaces, revealing a man who remains tied to his roots even as he builds a new life. However, he approaches these relationships with caution, aware that loyalty from the past does not guarantee trust in the present.

The complexity of Dwight's old relationships adds depth to his character, as he navigates the fine line between honoring his past and protecting his future. He is careful to avoid compromising his new empire in Tulsa, recognizing that his loyalty to those in his past cannot supersede his loyalty to those who stand by him now. Through these interactions, *Tulsa King* illustrates the difficulty of balancing old loyalties with new responsibilities, showing that while Dwight values his past, he's unwilling to sacrifice his future for relationships that may no longer serve him.

New Alliances in Tulsa: Building Loyalty from Scratch

In Tulsa, Dwight is tasked with building loyalty from scratch, a challenge that requires both patience and discernment. Figures like Bodhi, the bar owner; Mitch, the mechanic; and Tina, the young dealer, each represent new relationships that demand a different approach to loyalty. Unlike his life in New York, where loyalty was enforced through fear and tradition, Tulsa's independent operators need to feel respected and valued if they're to commit to Dwight's vision. This requires Dwight to adapt his leadership style, balancing authority with approachability.

Bodhi is one of Dwight's earliest allies, a figure whose cautious nature and reluctance to fully embrace Dwight's methods initially create tension. However, as Dwight proves his commitment to their partnership, Bodhi's loyalty deepens, transforming him from a hesitant collaborator to a trusted confidant. This evolution reflects Dwight's ability to foster loyalty by respecting Bodhi's independence, showing that he values Bodhi's input and respects his personal boundaries. Through Bodhi, *Tulsa King* highlights Dwight's adaptability, demonstrating that true loyalty is built not through control but through mutual respect and trust.

Similarly, Mitch's role as Dwight's logistical support is rooted in loyalty that is born from shared values and respect. Mitch appreciates Dwight's old-school principles and his willingness to protect those who work with him. In return, he offers Dwight unwavering loyalty, contributing his skills and resources to the operation. This relationship reflects the symbiotic nature of loyalty in Tulsa, where commitment is driven by a genuine belief in Dwight's vision rather than obligation or fear. Through Mitch, Dwight learns that loyalty in Tulsa is built on shared purpose, allowing him to create a network that feels less transactional and more personal.

Testing Loyalties: The Role of Conflict in Strengthening Bonds

Conflict plays a significant role in testing and solidifying loyalties within Dwight's network. The challenges Dwight faces—from rivals like Red to the scrutiny of local law enforcement—force his allies to make difficult choices, revealing the strength of their commitment to him. When faced with external threats, Dwight's allies are compelled to either stand by him or betray him, creating moments that define the depth of their loyalty. These conflicts serve as a crucible, allowing Dwight to identify those who are truly committed to his vision and those who may waver under pressure.

One example of this is Dwight's confrontations with Red's biker gang. When Red attempts to undermine Dwight's authority, it creates a situation where Dwight's allies must choose between supporting him or aligning with the more established local power. Through this conflict, Dwight is able to gauge the loyalty of individuals like Mitch and Tina, who stand by him even when faced with personal risk. These moments of loyalty reinforce the trust within his network, allowing Dwight to build an empire based on individuals who have proven their commitment through action.

Conflict also strengthens Dwight's relationship with law enforcement figures like Stacy. While their alliance is tenuous and unspoken, Stacy's willingness to look the other way demonstrates a level of respect and, to an extent, loyalty to Dwight's desire for stability in Tulsa. Their relationship is constantly tested by Stacy's duty to uphold the law and Dwight's need to protect his operation. This ongoing tension forces both to evaluate their priorities, creating a bond that is grounded in mutual understanding rather than overt allegiance. Through these interactions, Dwight learns that loyalty can come from unexpected places, even from those who are not directly aligned with his goals.

The Cost of Betrayal: Consequences and Lessons Learned

In *Tulsa King*, betrayal is not just a plot device; it's a formative experience that shapes Dwight's decisions and reinforces his understanding of loyalty's limits. Each act of betrayal he encounters serves as a painful reminder of the cost of misplaced trust, forcing him to refine his approach to leadership and trust. Dwight's response to betrayal is swift and uncompromising; he understands that allowing disloyalty to go unpunished would undermine his authority and weaken the loyalty of those who remain committed to him.

One notable example of betrayal comes from individuals who join Dwight's network only to pursue their own interests. These figures see Dwight's rise as an opportunity for profit rather than a commitment to his vision, and their betrayal forces him to reassess his recruitment strategy. By learning from these experiences, Dwight becomes more selective in his alliances, valuing quality over quantity and prioritizing individuals who demonstrate genuine loyalty. This lesson reinforces his belief that loyalty cannot be assumed; it must be earned through mutual respect and proven commitment.

The cost of betrayal also extends to Dwight's personal growth, as he learns to balance trust with caution. His past has taught him the importance of loyalty, but his experiences in Tulsa reveal the need for discernment. By confronting betrayal head-on, Dwight gains a deeper understanding of the complexities of loyalty, recognizing that true allegiance comes from shared values rather than blind faith. Through these painful lessons, he becomes a more resilient and strategic leader, capable of navigating the treacherous waters of Tulsa's underworld without compromising his principles.

Building a Legacy Through Loyalty: Dwight's Vision for Tulsa

Ultimately, Dwight's journey is about more than power or influence; it's about building a legacy based on loyalty and mutual respect. He understands that an empire built on fear alone is fragile, susceptible to betrayal and rebellion. In Tulsa, Dwight has the opportunity to create something lasting, a network that reflects his values and serves as a testament to his commitment to loyalty. This vision shapes his interactions with his allies, as he seeks to cultivate a network that is bound not by obligation but by genuine respect and shared purpose.

Through his relationships with figures like Bodhi, Mitch, and Tina, Dwight creates a community that values loyalty as much as he does, fostering a sense of unity that goes beyond profit or power. His approach to loyalty is not one-sided; he offers protection, support, and guidance to those who align with him, treating them as family rather than pawns. This reciprocal loyalty allows Dwight to build an empire that feels personal and meaningful, a legacy that reflects his journey of redemption and reinvention.

In Tulsa, Dwight's loyalty becomes both his greatest strength and his most enduring legacy. By creating a network built on trust and respect, he demonstrates that true power comes not from fear but from unity, proving that even in the darkest realms of the underworld, loyalty can be a source of light. Through his commitment to loyalty, Dwight builds a new kind of empire, one that reflects his evolution as a leader and his belief that loyalty, when reciprocated, is the foundation of any lasting legacy.

Conclusion: Loyalty and Betrayal in the Making of a King

In *Tulsa King*, loyalty and betrayal are more than just themes; they are the forces that shape Dwight Manfredi's journey and define his relationships. Dwight's unwavering commitment to loyalty serves as both his guiding principle and his greatest vulnerability, as he learns that true allegiance is rare and often hard-won. Through his experiences in Tulsa, Dwight discovers that loyalty is a two-way street, one that requires mutual respect, trust, and a willingness to protect those who stand by him.

Betrayal, on the other hand, serves as a painful but necessary reminder of loyalty's limitations. Each act of disloyalty teaches Dwight valuable lessons about discernment, trust, and resilience, allowing him to build a network that is both strong and loyal. Through these experiences, Dwight becomes a more strategic and compassionate leader, learning that true loyalty is born not from fear but from genuine respect and shared purpose.

As Dwight builds his empire in Tulsa, he transforms loyalty from a personal value into the cornerstone of his legacy. By fostering a network of allies who share his vision, he creates an empire that reflects his commitment to loyalty, unity, and mutual respect. In the end, Dwight's journey in *Tulsa King* is a testament to the power of loyalty and the strength that comes from facing betrayal, proving that even in a world marked by treachery, loyalty remains the foundation of any true king's rule.

Chapter 14: Tension and Conflict
Introduction: A World Defined by Tension and Conflict

In *Tulsa King*, tension and conflict are woven into every interaction, plot twist, and character arc, creating a story that keeps viewers on edge. For Dwight "The General" Manfredi, every decision carries risk, every ally has their own agenda, and every day presents new challenges. Whether he's contending with rivals, balancing alliances, or managing the inherent instability of a small-town criminal network, Dwight's journey is defined by an undercurrent of tension that propels the story forward. Each moment of conflict tests his loyalty, resilience, and cunning, making his journey in Tulsa a relentless game of survival.

This chapter explores the key moments of tension and conflict in *Tulsa King*, examining how these scenes not only keep viewers engaged but also reveal new dimensions of Dwight's character and the dangerous world he inhabits. From confrontations with rivals to moral dilemmas, these moments of tension are essential to the show's atmosphere, offering a glimpse into the high-stakes reality of Dwight's life as he builds his empire.

Initial Confrontation with Red and the Biker Gang

One of the earliest and most pivotal conflicts Dwight faces in Tulsa is his encounter with Red and his biker gang, a faction that controls a portion of Tulsa's drug trade and other illegal activities. From the moment Dwight arrives, Red views him as an outsider and a threat to his territory. Unlike Dwight, who operates with a calculated and respectful approach to power, Red relies on intimidation and brute force, seeing himself as the dominant force in Tulsa's underworld. Their clash is inevitable, setting the stage for an ongoing rivalry that brings tension to every corner of Dwight's operation.

This initial confrontation is a defining moment for Dwight. In one intense scene, Red and his gang attempt to intimidate Dwight, testing his resolve and pushing him to respond. Dwight, who is both older and more seasoned, meets their aggression with a calm but steely demeanor, signaling that he won't be easily intimidated. The tension in this moment is palpable; viewers know that any misstep could lead to a violent escalation. But instead of reacting with violence, Dwight uses his presence and reputation to assert control, letting Red know that he's not to be underestimated.

This encounter sets the tone for Dwight's relationship with Red and his gang, establishing a dynamic of mutual hostility tempered by begrudging respect. The ongoing conflict with Red becomes a constant source of tension in the series, as both men vie for control over Tulsa's underworld. Each encounter between them serves as a reminder of the fragile balance Dwight must maintain, highlighting his ability to navigate hostility with a mix of strategy, patience, and strength. This rivalry also underscores Dwight's adaptability, as he learns to manage a local adversary whose methods differ greatly from the organized crime tactics he's accustomed to.

Building an Empire Under the Watchful Eye of Law Enforcement

While Dwight is skilled at avoiding detection, his efforts in Tulsa do not go unnoticed by local law enforcement, adding another layer of tension to the series. Stacy, a diligent and perceptive police officer, quickly becomes aware of Dwight's presence and the influence he's starting to exert over the community. Though she doesn't have concrete evidence, her instincts tell her that Dwight is more than just a new face in town. This dynamic creates a cat-and-mouse game, as Dwight must conduct his operations discreetly, all while staying one step ahead of Stacy's suspicions.

The tension between Dwight and Stacy reaches a peak during their chance meetings, where each interaction is laced with unspoken threats and thinly veiled intentions. Dwight is careful to maintain a polite, even friendly demeanor, recognizing that Stacy's attention could spell trouble for his operation. Meanwhile, Stacy probes subtly, trying to get a sense of his activities without openly accusing him. This dynamic is marked by a constant, simmering tension, as both characters are aware of each other's agendas but constrained by the lack of concrete evidence. For viewers, these scenes offer a nerve-wracking balance between suspicion and subtle manipulation, highlighting Dwight's ability to manage threats from both criminal and legal fronts.

The pressure of law enforcement oversight forces Dwight to make strategic decisions that could either protect his operation or expose it to further scrutiny. Every encounter with Stacy is a reminder of the risk he faces, as even the slightest slip could jeopardize everything he has built. This tension is heightened by Dwight's recognition that Stacy is both intelligent and dedicated, a formidable opponent who won't be easily swayed. The ongoing tension between Dwight and Stacy creates a backdrop of constant surveillance, underscoring the precariousness of Dwight's position and adding a level of suspense that keeps viewers engaged.

Betrayals Within His Inner Circle

As Dwight's operation grows, he faces the inevitable challenge of betrayal from within his own ranks. While he prides himself on fostering loyalty among his allies, the nature of organized crime means that trust is often a rare commodity. Figures within his network, particularly those driven by personal gain or fear of repercussions, occasionally waver in their allegiance. These moments of betrayal are not only a source of tension but also a test of Dwight's judgment and resilience, as he must confront the reality that even those closest to him can become threats.

One of the most gripping moments of betrayal comes from a seemingly loyal associate who, tempted by a rival's offer, begins leaking information about Dwight's operation. When Dwight discovers the betrayal, the tension escalates, as he must decide how to handle the disloyalty without sending shockwaves through his network. The scene where Dwight confronts the traitor is intense, marked by an undercurrent of anger tempered by his need for control. Rather than resorting to impulsive violence, Dwight's response is calculated, showcasing his ability to handle betrayal in a way that maintains his authority without destabilizing his network.

These instances of betrayal force Dwight to constantly evaluate the loyalty of those around him, adding a layer of suspense to his every interaction. Viewers are left on edge, aware that any one of his associates could turn against him under the right (or wrong) circumstances. These betrayals not only create dramatic tension but also highlight Dwight's adaptability, as he learns to manage his empire with a balance of trust and vigilance, reinforcing his understanding that loyalty in the underworld is rarely absolute.

The High-Stakes Conflict with Rival Gangs and Criminals

As Dwight's influence grows, he inevitably attracts the attention of rival factions beyond Red's biker gang. These independent criminals and small-time operators see Dwight as both a competitor and a threat to their autonomy, sparking conflicts that escalate the tension within Tulsa's underworld. These rivalries are not merely territorial; they're ideological, with each faction viewing Dwight's presence as an intrusion on their established operations. For Dwight, these conflicts are a reminder of the relentless nature of his work, as he must assert his authority without sparking an all-out war.

One of the most intense conflicts arises when a rival gang attempts to disrupt one of Dwight's key transactions, hoping to weaken his influence and deter future expansion. The scene is a high-stakes standoff, with each side aware that the slightest miscalculation could lead to violence. Dwight, ever the strategist, manages to de-escalate the situation, turning the tables on his rivals with a mix of calculated threats and negotiation. This tense exchange reveals his ability to control conflict, showcasing his skill in managing hostile situations without compromising his authority.

These rivalries create ongoing tension in the series, as Dwight's expansion inevitably provokes resistance from those who resent his influence. Each confrontation is a test of his leadership, as he must balance his need for control with the risks of open conflict. These scenes of tension and conflict serve as powerful reminders of the precarious nature of Dwight's empire, where every gain is matched by new threats, and every victory is met with fresh challenges.

Confronting His Moral Dilemmas: Loyalty Versus Survival

Dwight's journey is not only shaped by external conflicts but also by internal struggles, as he grapples with moral dilemmas that challenge his loyalty and sense of honor. These moments of tension are deeply personal, revealing the complexity of Dwight's character and the conflicts that define his code of ethics. Throughout the series, Dwight is faced with choices that force him to weigh his loyalty to those he trusts against his need for self-preservation and success. These moral conflicts add a layer of psychological tension, highlighting the emotional toll of his lifestyle and the sacrifices required to survive in the underworld.

One of the most poignant moments of moral tension arises when Dwight is forced to choose between protecting a close ally and advancing his operation. His decision is fraught with consequences; if he chooses loyalty, he risks exposing his network to scrutiny and losing valuable resources. If he prioritizes survival, he may lose the trust and respect of his inner circle. This internal conflict is portrayed with a level of intensity that resonates deeply with viewers, as Dwight's struggle reflects the human cost of his lifestyle. His ultimate decision showcases his loyalty, but it also reveals the vulnerability that comes with living by a personal code in a world that rarely rewards honor.

These moral dilemmas create a psychological tension that runs parallel to Dwight's external conflicts, providing viewers with insight into the complexity of his character. His willingness to wrestle with these choices demonstrates his depth, as he's not merely a leader driven by power but a man shaped by values and personal convictions. These moments of internal conflict add emotional weight to the series, reminding viewers that Dwight's journey is as much about his own redemption as it is about building an empire.

The Constant Threat of Exposure and Arrest

As Dwight builds his empire, the looming threat of exposure and arrest becomes an ever-present source of tension. With law enforcement watching his every move and rival factions eager to see him fail, Dwight must navigate a landscape where one misstep could bring everything crashing down. This constant pressure is amplified by the surveillance and digital tracking that pervade modern society, making it nearly impossible to avoid detection entirely. Dwight's awareness of these risks forces him to operate with extreme caution, creating a tension that permeates his every action.

One of the most suspenseful moments of the series occurs when a minor slip in his operation draws the attention of federal investigators, threatening to unravel his entire network. This high-stakes scenario forces Dwight to act quickly, devising a plan to divert attention while securing his assets and allies. The intensity of this moment is heightened by the knowledge that even a minor mistake could bring his entire operation to light, highlighting the delicate balance Dwight must maintain between ambition and caution.

The threat of exposure serves as a constant reminder of the risks inherent in Dwight's lifestyle, adding a layer of suspense that keeps viewers on edge. Each decision, each move, carries the potential for disaster, forcing Dwight to operate with a level of precision that leaves no room for error. This ongoing tension between success and exposure defines the stakes of Dwight's journey, reinforcing the reality that power in the underworld is always accompanied by the risk of ruin.

Climaxing Confrontations: High-Stakes Showdowns

As the series progresses, the tension and conflict culminate in high-stakes showdowns that test Dwight's strength, strategy, and resilience. These climactic moments bring all of his challenges to a head, pitting him against his most formidable rivals in battles that are as psychological as they are physical. Each showdown serves as a turning point, marking a shift in Dwight's journey and reinforcing the stakes of his quest for control.

One of the most memorable climactic confrontations involves Dwight facing off against Red and his biker gang in a final bid for dominance. The intensity of the scene is heightened by the anticipation that has built up over the season, with viewers aware that this confrontation has been inevitable from the start. Dwight's approach to the showdown is strategic, leveraging both his allies and his experience to outmaneuver Red. The tension is palpable as each man attempts to assert control, culminating in a resolution that redefines Dwight's place in Tulsa's underworld.

These climactic confrontations are not only thrilling but also deeply revealing, showcasing Dwight's evolution as a leader and his ability to overcome adversity. Each showdown reflects the cumulative impact of the challenges he has faced, highlighting his resilience and his commitment to building a legacy. These high-stakes moments are the payoff for the tension that has permeated the series, offering viewers a sense of resolution while leaving room for new conflicts to emerge.

Conclusion: The Role of Tension and Conflict in Dwight's Journey

In *Tulsa King*, tension and conflict are the lifeblood of the narrative, driving the story forward and adding depth to Dwight Manfredi's journey. From confrontations with rivals to internal struggles, each moment of conflict reveals new dimensions of Dwight's character and the challenges he faces in building his empire. These scenes of tension are not merely thrilling; they serve as essential components of Dwight's evolution, testing his loyalty, resilience, and strategic acumen.

Through each moment of tension and conflict, viewers gain insight into the complexity of Dwight's world, where power is always accompanied by risk and loyalty is tested at every turn. The stakes are high, the challenges relentless, and the choices fraught with consequence. As Dwight navigates this dangerous landscape, he becomes a figure defined not only by his ambition but by his ability to thrive in a world marked by uncertainty, danger, and the ever-present threat of betrayal.

In *Tulsa King*, tension and conflict are more than just sources of suspense; they are the forces that shape Dwight's destiny, proving that true power is earned not through victory alone but through the courage to face every challenge with unwavering resolve.

Chapter 15: Comparisons to Stallone's Iconic Roles
Introduction: The Evolution of a Legend

Sylvester Stallone has created some of cinema's most enduring characters, from the underdog boxer Rocky Balboa to the relentless war hero John Rambo. Each character Stallone has portrayed over his decades-long career has left an indelible mark on audiences, symbolizing resilience, grit, and the fight for personal redemption. With *Tulsa King*, Stallone adds Dwight "The General" Manfredi to his pantheon of iconic roles, a character who draws on the traits of his predecessors yet carves out a unique identity shaped by loyalty, strategy, and a complex moral code. Dwight's journey in *Tulsa King* reflects Stallone's ability to evolve as an actor, taking on a character who is as layered and introspective as he is powerful and resilient.

This chapter explores how Dwight "The General" Manfredi stacks up against Stallone's iconic characters, examining the similarities, differences, and the ways in which this role marks a significant evolution in Stallone's portrayal of masculinity, leadership, and redemption. Through Dwight, Stallone brings a new dimension to his repertoire, portraying a character who combines the toughness of his past heroes with the wisdom and introspection that come from years of experience and hard-won resilience.

Rocky Balboa: The Fighter with an Underdog Spirit

One of Stallone's most famous roles, Rocky Balboa, is defined by his underdog status, relentless determination, and the heart he brings to every fight. Like Rocky, Dwight Manfredi is an outsider—albeit in a different way—navigating a world that is unfamiliar, inhospitable, and often openly hostile. While Rocky's journey is one of physical endurance and the will to rise against the odds, Dwight's journey in *Tulsa King* is more cerebral, focusing on strategy and the resilience required to build an empire in a new land. However, both characters share a deep-seated commitment to honor and integrity, making them men of principle in worlds that often lack such qualities.

In many ways, Dwight's loyalty and sense of responsibility to those around him echo Rocky's devotion to his family, friends, and community. Just as Rocky fights to provide for Adrian and his loved ones, Dwight's commitment to his allies in Tulsa shows his desire to protect and uplift those who stand by him. This sense of loyalty is central to both characters, as they view relationships as sacred and are willing to fight—and, if necessary, sacrifice—for the people they care about.

Yet, while Rocky remains an optimist at heart, Dwight carries the weight of past betrayals and a more cynical outlook shaped by his time in prison and experiences in organized crime. Unlike Rocky, who approaches life with a sense of innocence and hope, Dwight is hardened, cautious, and strategic. This difference highlights the evolution of Stallone's portrayal of resilience. Dwight's journey is less about redemption through fighting and more about survival through wisdom and calculated risk, showcasing Stallone's growth as an actor who can bring depth and subtlety to a character shaped by years of experience and hardship.

John Rambo: The Reluctant Warrior and Lone Survivor

John Rambo, the hardened war veteran from the *Rambo* series, is another of Stallone's iconic roles, defined by his unmatched survival skills, lone-wolf mentality, and struggle with inner demons. Like Rambo, Dwight is a survivor, a man who has endured unimaginable hardship and emerges with a fierce determination to rebuild his life. Both characters are reluctant heroes, men who are drawn into conflict not by choice but by necessity, forced to rely on their strength and cunning to navigate hostile environments.

Where Rambo's journey is one of physical survival in literal battlefields, Dwight's survival skills are tested in the figurative battlefield of Tulsa's underworld. Dwight's experience in the criminal world mirrors Rambo's military experience, equipping him with a skill set that allows him to assess danger, adapt to new threats, and operate independently when necessary. However, unlike Rambo, who remains isolated and often misunderstood, Dwight actively seeks to build a network and establish connections, using his influence to unite rather than destroy. This difference reveals a softer, more relational side to Dwight, one that distinguishes him from the lone-wolf image of Rambo.

Additionally, Dwight's journey toward redemption is more personal and introspective than Rambo's. While Rambo is haunted by the horrors of war and struggles to reintegrate into society, Dwight is motivated by a desire to make amends, to leave a legacy that reflects his values rather than his past mistakes. In this sense, Dwight represents an evolution of the warrior archetype, a character who uses his resilience not only for survival but to build something meaningful. Through Dwight, Stallone portrays a warrior who is not just fighting external battles but is also on a quest for inner peace, highlighting his ability to bring nuance and depth to a character shaped by both trauma and hope for the future.

Judge Dredd: The Lawman with a Strict Moral Code

In *Judge Dredd*, Stallone portrays a character who is bound by an unyielding sense of justice, operating in a world where order and control are paramount. Judge Dredd's view of justice is absolute; he follows the law to the letter, seeing no room for negotiation or compromise. While Dwight does not share Judge Dredd's role as a literal lawman, he operates with a similar sense of duty and a personal code of ethics that guides his actions. For Dwight, loyalty, respect, and honor are non-negotiable, principles that he adheres to even as he operates outside the law.

However, unlike Judge Dredd's rigid adherence to authority, Dwight's moral code is flexible, shaped by years of experience and a nuanced understanding of human nature. While Dredd's black-and-white view of justice often leads him to act without mercy, Dwight understands the value of compassion, loyalty, and even forgiveness when it serves a greater purpose. This evolution in Stallone's portrayal of morality is significant, as it shows his ability to play a character who operates in moral gray areas without losing his sense of integrity.

Dwight's approach to power and authority also contrasts with Judge Dredd's. Where Dredd enforces his will through sheer authority, Dwight builds loyalty through respect, treating his allies as equals rather than subordinates. This difference reflects Dwight's understanding that true influence comes from connection rather than control, highlighting Stallone's ability to portray a leader who values relationships over dominance. Through Dwight, Stallone explores a more nuanced form of leadership, one that recognizes the importance of collaboration, trust, and mutual respect.

Marion "Cobra" Cobretti: The Enforcer with a Reluctant Heart

In *Cobra*, Stallone's character, Marion "Cobra" Cobretti, is a tough, no-nonsense cop who takes justice into his own hands, often using brute force to deal with criminals. Cobretti's approach to justice is uncompromising, reflecting his belief that violence is sometimes necessary to restore order. While Dwight shares Cobretti's readiness to act decisively when the situation demands it, his approach to conflict is far more calculated. Dwight views violence as a last resort, a tool to be used sparingly and only when necessary.

Dwight's restraint contrasts with Cobretti's more impulsive approach, reflecting the wisdom and discipline that come with age and experience. Unlike Cobretti, who often operates on instinct, Dwight is deliberate in his decisions, weighing the potential consequences of each action. This difference reveals a new dimension of Stallone's acting, as he portrays a character who is not driven solely by the need to assert power but by a desire to build something meaningful. Dwight's approach to conflict demonstrates Stallone's ability to embody a character who values strategy over force, showing that true strength lies in the ability to remain calm and controlled even in the face of danger.

Moreover, while Cobretti is a character defined by his role as an enforcer, Dwight's journey is one of transformation. He is not just enforcing a code; he is creating a legacy, shaping his world according to principles that reflect his values. This evolution in Stallone's portrayal of the "enforcer" archetype highlights his growth as an actor, as he brings depth to a character who understands that power is not just about control but about leaving a positive impact on those who follow him.

Lincoln Hawk in *Over the Top*: The Reluctant Father Figure

In *Over the Top*, Stallone plays Lincoln Hawk, a truck driver and arm-wrestling champion who fights to reconnect with his estranged son. Hawk's journey is one of redemption, as he seeks to prove his love and commitment despite the odds stacked against him. Like Hawk, Dwight exhibits a paternal instinct, often acting as a mentor and protector to those in his circle. His relationship with figures like Tina and Mitch reflects this fatherly role, as he guides them, protects them, and even teaches them the values that have shaped his own life.

Dwight's role as a father figure brings a softer side to his character, showing that he is more than just a mob boss; he is someone who genuinely cares about the well-being of those he leads. This paternal instinct is similar to Lincoln Hawk's, as both characters find meaning in guiding the next generation and offering support to those in need. Through Dwight, Stallone explores the theme of redemption through mentorship, portraying a character who seeks to make amends by imparting wisdom and protecting those who rely on him.

However, unlike Hawk, whose journey is primarily about personal redemption, Dwight's journey is as much about building a legacy as it is about healing his past. His role as a mentor is not limited to a single individual; he is creating a network, a community that embodies his principles and reflects his growth as a leader. This difference highlights Stallone's ability to portray a character who balances personal relationships with a broader sense of purpose, showing that true redemption comes not only from individual acts but from creating a lasting impact.

Freddy Heflin in *Cop Land*: The Aging Figure Seeking Redemption

In *Cop Land*, Stallone plays Freddy Heflin, a small-town sheriff who finds himself caught in a web of corruption and must confront his own moral compass. Freddy, like Dwight, is a character searching for redemption, wrestling with his past mistakes and seeking to make things right. Both characters are older, more introspective figures who have endured hardship and are driven by a need for personal atonement. Dwight's journey in *Tulsa King* reflects a similar desire for redemption, as he seeks to build an empire that aligns with his values rather than repeating the mistakes of his past.

Where Freddy is limited by his physical and emotional scars, Dwight's experience in organized crime gives him a unique strength, allowing him to navigate the complexities of Tulsa's underworld with a sense of purpose. However, both characters share a vulnerability, a willingness to confront their flaws and strive for something better. Through Dwight, Stallone portrays a character who, like Freddy, is motivated by a sense of duty to himself and those he cares about, showing that true strength comes from facing one's past with honesty and resilience.

Dwight's journey of redemption, like Freddy's, is one of self-discovery, as he learns to balance his need for power with his desire for peace. This evolution in Stallone's portrayal of the "redeemed hero" archetype showcases his ability to bring depth and empathy to characters who are shaped by their pasts but not defined by them. Through Dwight, Stallone explores the complexity of redemption, portraying a man who understands that making amends is a journey, one that requires both strength and humility.

Conclusion: Dwight Manfredi as the Culmination of Stallone's Career

Dwight "The General" Manfredi in *Tulsa King* is not only a new character in Stallone's repertoire but a culmination of his career, embodying the resilience, loyalty, wisdom, and complexity that have defined his most iconic roles. Through Dwight, Stallone brings together the physical strength of Rocky, the survival instincts of Rambo, the moral code of Judge Dredd, the discipline of Cobra, the fatherly compassion of Lincoln Hawk, and the quest for redemption of Freddy Heflin. Dwight is a character who carries the weight of Stallone's past roles while adding a new layer of introspection, strategy, and adaptability.

In *Tulsa King*, Stallone showcases his ability to evolve as an actor, portraying a character who is as much defined by his flaws as he is by his strengths. Dwight is a man who understands the complexities of loyalty, the value of resilience, and the importance of leaving a legacy that reflects his principles. Through Dwight, Stallone offers audiences a character who is both powerful and vulnerable, a leader who understands that true strength comes not from domination but from connection, wisdom, and the willingness to adapt.

Dwight "The General" Manfredi stands as a testament to Stallone's growth as an actor and storyteller, a character who honors the legacy of Stallone's iconic roles while carving out a new path that reflects the actor's own journey. In Dwight, Stallone has created a character who is not only a reflection of his past but a symbol of his evolution, proving that even the most seasoned heroes can find new ways to inspire, captivate, and resonate with audiences.

Chapter 16: The Show's Cinematic Quality
Introduction: Bringing Cinematic Brilliance to the Small Screen

Tulsa King distinguishes itself not only through its storyline and character development but also through its stunning visual style, which gives the series a movie-like quality that draws viewers deeply into Dwight Manfredi's world. With carefully crafted cinematography, dynamic shot compositions, atmospheric lighting, and attention to detail, the series captures the gritty beauty of Tulsa's landscapes, the intensity of its underworld, and the raw emotions of its characters. Each scene is treated as a standalone moment of visual storytelling, making the show feel more like a cinematic experience than a traditional television series.

The show's cinematography and visual style serve as more than mere backdrop; they actively contribute to the narrative, enhancing the tension, drama, and depth of Dwight's journey. By blending elements of neo-Western and crime thriller aesthetics, *Tulsa King* creates a unique visual identity that resonates with viewers, transporting them to a world where every shadow, street corner, and cityscape holds meaning. This chapter delves into the elements of cinematography and visual design that give *Tulsa King* its cinematic quality, exploring how these techniques elevate the series and bring an added layer of immersion to Dwight's story.

Capturing Tulsa's Landscape: A Character of Its Own

One of the most striking aspects of *Tulsa King* is its portrayal of Tulsa itself, a city that becomes as much a character in the show as Dwight and his associates. Through wide, sweeping shots of open plains, expansive highways, and rustic buildings, the cinematography brings the rugged beauty of Oklahoma to life, creating a setting that is both haunting and compelling. This backdrop reflects Dwight's journey, as he is thrust into an unfamiliar land with its own rhythm, culture, and hidden dangers. The landscape becomes a mirror for Dwight's isolation and his determination to build something meaningful in a world that is as harsh as it is beautiful.

The use of drone shots and aerial views offers viewers a perspective of Tulsa that highlights its mix of rural and urban, a blend that is rare in most crime dramas. These wide shots create a sense of openness that contrasts with the confined, high-stakes world of New York that Dwight left behind. By capturing the vastness of the landscape, the cinematography emphasizes Dwight's sense of being a stranger in a strange land, creating a visual metaphor for his journey. The sprawling landscapes suggest opportunity and danger in equal measure, reflecting Dwight's mission to carve out a place for himself in this unfamiliar territory.

Additionally, Tulsa's buildings, streets, and dive bars are filmed with a gritty realism that highlights the city's character. Locations like Bodhi's bar, Mitch's garage, and the dimly lit alleyways of Tulsa add an atmosphere of raw authenticity, making viewers feel as though they are experiencing the town through Dwight's eyes. The cinematography captures the textures of worn brick, neon lights, and dusty roads, imbuing the series with a sense of place that grounds the story. By treating Tulsa as a living, breathing character, the show's visual style immerses viewers in the setting, making every interaction and location feel essential to the narrative.

Lighting and Color Palette: A Neo-Western Aesthetic

Tulsa King uses lighting and color to establish a visual style that draws from the neo-Western genre, infusing the series with a sense of ruggedness and Americana that complements Dwight's storyline. The color palette is dominated by earthy tones—rusty browns, deep blues, and muted grays—that reflect the dusty, raw environment of Tulsa. This color scheme reinforces the show's gritty atmosphere, creating a world that feels grounded, real, and tinged with a sense of nostalgia. The use of warm and cold colors also enhances the emotional tone of each scene, reflecting Dwight's inner conflicts and the shifting dynamics of his relationships.

Lighting plays a crucial role in setting the mood, with dimly lit interiors and stark, sun-drenched exteriors capturing the extremes of Dwight's new environment. In scenes set in darkened bars, garages, or back rooms, the lighting is minimal, often casting shadows that heighten the tension and mystery. These shadows serve as visual representations of Dwight's complex relationships, where trust and betrayal are constantly at play. By using low lighting and strategic shadows, the cinematography reflects the secrecy and danger inherent in Dwight's world, making each interaction feel like a high-stakes encounter.

In contrast, scenes shot in the open, sunlit streets of Tulsa provide a sense of clarity and openness, creating a visual dichotomy between Dwight's public and private worlds. The harsh sunlight of Oklahoma is captured in all its intensity, illuminating the landscape in a way that feels both beautiful and unforgiving. This lighting choice reflects Dwight's vulnerability in Tulsa, as he navigates a world where every move is visible and every decision is scrutinized. The interplay of light and shadow adds depth to Dwight's character, illustrating his struggle to balance his need for discretion with his desire to establish a visible legacy.

Cinematic Framing and Shot Composition: Elevating the Narrative

The framing and shot composition in *Tulsa King* elevate the storytelling, using visual cues to communicate the underlying themes and conflicts in Dwight's journey. From close-ups that capture Dwight's expressions to wide shots that place him in the vast landscape of Tulsa, each frame is carefully composed to enhance the emotional and narrative weight of the scene. The series often employs a symmetrical framing style, positioning Dwight at the center of the frame to convey his power and presence. This composition gives Dwight a commanding presence, even in moments of solitude, reflecting his determination and his sense of purpose.

Close-up shots are used strategically to capture the subtleties of Dwight's expressions, allowing viewers to see the internal struggles he faces as he navigates new alliances and confrontations. These shots create a sense of intimacy, inviting viewers to connect with Dwight on a personal level, understanding his motivations, doubts, and resilience. By focusing on the minutiae of his expressions, the cinematography reveals the depth of Dwight's character, highlighting his humanity even as he operates in a ruthless world.

In contrast, wide shots and long takes are used to underscore the scale and isolation of Dwight's environment. When Dwight is shown walking through empty streets, vast fields, or quiet neighborhoods, the framing emphasizes his outsider status, creating a visual representation of his exile from New York. These expansive shots convey a sense of isolation that mirrors Dwight's journey, showing that despite his influence, he is still a man far from home, forced to build an empire in a land where he is a stranger. By combining close-ups with wide shots, the cinematography creates a rhythm that balances Dwight's personal struggle with the broader narrative, giving viewers a cinematic experience that feels both epic and intimate.

Action Sequences and Tension: A Gritty Realism

The action sequences in *Tulsa King* are filmed with a gritty realism that reflects the series' grounded approach to violence and conflict. Unlike the choreographed, polished fights of traditional action films, the show's action scenes are raw and unrefined, capturing the unpredictability and brutality of real confrontations. The cinematography in these scenes uses handheld cameras and quick cuts to create a sense of immediacy, making viewers feel as though they are part of the action. This style emphasizes the stakes of each conflict, as Dwight is often forced to rely on his instincts and experience rather than brute strength alone.

One of the most effective techniques used in action sequences is the use of tight framing, which keeps the focus on Dwight and his opponent, intensifying the physicality of the fight. The camera movements are quick and often shaky, mirroring the adrenaline and chaos of the moment. This approach makes the action feel visceral and grounded, a stark contrast to the stylized violence often seen in other crime dramas.

The use of close-ups and fast cuts heightens the impact of each blow, creating a sense of realism that underscores the dangers Dwight faces.

In addition to hand-to-hand combat, the series also uses wide shots and long takes to build tension before moments of confrontation. By showing Dwight and his adversaries approaching each other from a distance, the cinematography creates a slow-burning suspense, allowing viewers to anticipate the coming conflict. This deliberate pacing adds a cinematic quality to the action, treating each encounter as a high-stakes showdown that reflects the Western influence on the series' visual style. By combining gritty realism with cinematic pacing, *Tulsa King* delivers action sequences that feel intense and authentic, capturing the raw power and vulnerability of Dwight's world.

Symbolism and Visual Metaphors: Adding Depth to Dwight's Journey

The cinematography in *Tulsa King* goes beyond simply capturing the story; it uses symbolism and visual metaphors to add layers of meaning to Dwight's journey. The show frequently uses mirrors, reflections, and other visual motifs to illustrate Dwight's internal struggles and the duality of his character. For instance, scenes where Dwight is shown in reflection, such as in a mirror or window, underscore his introspective nature, hinting at the contrast between his past self and the man he is trying to become in Tulsa. These moments serve as visual representations of Dwight's search for redemption and self-acceptance, adding depth to his character arc.

Color is also used symbolically to represent Dwight's journey. In scenes where he is grappling with moral dilemmas or moments of vulnerability, the colors are often subdued, with muted grays and dark blues dominating the palette. This color choice reflects the weight of Dwight's past and the uncertainty of his future. In contrast, scenes that depict moments of success, alliance, or triumph are often infused with warmer tones, suggesting hope and the possibility of a new beginning. These shifts in color subtly communicate Dwight's evolving mindset, offering viewers insight into his emotional landscape.

Furthermore, the cinematography frequently juxtaposes Dwight's presence against the vastness of the Oklahoma landscape, using wide shots to convey a sense of scale and perspective. These scenes visually communicate Dwight's insignificance within the larger world, reminding viewers that despite his power and influence, he is still a man contending with forces beyond his control. By placing Dwight within the vast expanse of Tulsa's environment, the cinematography reinforces the themes of isolation, resilience, and ambition that drive his character.

Neo-Noir Influences: Shadows and Light in Dwight's World

Drawing from the neo-noir genre, *Tulsa King* uses shadow and light to create an atmosphere of mystery and moral ambiguity that complements Dwight's complex character. The series often frames Dwight in partial shadow, using darkness to symbolize the secrets he carries and the dangers that surround him. This play of light and shadow reflects the duality of his world, where allies can turn to enemies, and every decision carries the risk of betrayal. By immersing Dwight in shadow, the cinematography highlights the tension between his loyalty to his code and the compromises he must make to survive.

Low-key lighting is particularly prominent in indoor scenes, such as the back rooms of bars, garages, and dimly lit meeting spaces where Dwight conducts his business. These environments are filled with shadows, creating a sense of claustrophobia and uncertainty that mirrors the secrecy and risk of Dwight's lifestyle. The neo-noir lighting enhances the show's gritty tone, imbuing each scene with an air of mystery and danger that keeps viewers on edge.

In contrast, moments of clarity or revelation are often accompanied by a shift in lighting, with brighter, more direct illumination bringing Dwight's face into focus. This technique visually represents Dwight's moments of self-awareness and his struggle to define his own path amidst the darkness of his past. By using light and shadow to reflect Dwight's internal journey, the cinematography adds a psychological depth to the series, revealing the complexities of his character and the ethical challenges he faces.

Conclusion: A Cinematic Experience on the Small Screen

Tulsa King achieves a level of cinematic quality that elevates it from a typical crime drama to an immersive visual experience. Through its detailed cinematography, atmospheric lighting, symbolic use of color, and neo-noir influences, the show creates a world that feels both vast and intimate, capturing the intricacies of Dwight Manfredi's journey with a level of artistry that rivals feature films. Each scene is meticulously crafted, treating the landscape, characters, and moments of tension as essential components of a visual story that resonates with viewers on multiple levels.

The show's commitment to visual storytelling is a testament to the creative vision behind *Tulsa King*, as it uses cinematography not merely as a backdrop but as a narrative tool that enhances the story's emotional and thematic depth. By blending neo-Western and noir aesthetics, the series crafts a unique visual identity that immerses viewers in Dwight's world, making them feel the weight of his decisions, the dangers of his lifestyle, and the beauty of the world he inhabits.

Through its cinematic quality, *Tulsa King* demonstrates that television can achieve the scope and artistry of cinema, proving that great storytelling is not limited by format. In Dwight's journey, the show finds a balance between action, introspection, and visual symbolism, offering audiences a story that is as captivating to watch as it is to follow. By combining stunning visuals with a compelling narrative, *Tulsa King* stands as a masterclass in cinematic television, a series that invites viewers to lose themselves in a world that is as dangerous as it is beautiful, as vast as it is personal.

Chapter 17: Character Growth Throughout the Series
Introduction: A Journey of Transformation

In *Tulsa King*, Dwight "The General" Manfredi is more than a mafia capo with a mission; he is a character in constant evolution, shaped by his past and adapting to his new life in Tulsa. When we first meet Dwight, he is a man defined by loyalty, resilience, and a sense of duty forged in the world of organized crime. But as the series progresses, his character undergoes a profound transformation, moving from a hardened mobster to a figure of influence, wisdom, and introspection. This journey is not only about building an empire but also about personal redemption, self-discovery, and the search for a meaningful legacy.

Throughout the series, Dwight's growth is marked by key moments of conflict, relationship-building, and self-reflection that reveal new dimensions of his character. This chapter traces Dwight's development, examining how each experience shapes his identity and ultimately transforms him into a leader who values loyalty, honor, and purpose over sheer power.

Early Days in Tulsa: A Man Out of His Element

When Dwight first arrives in Tulsa, he is out of his element, a seasoned New York mobster transplanted into a small-town environment that operates by different rules. His initial interactions with the locals, from Bodhi to Mitch, reveal a man who is both adaptable and determined to assert his influence, even if his tactics sometimes clash with Tulsa's unstructured underworld. Dwight's initial approach is marked by confidence and an unyielding sense of control; he expects people to follow his lead without question, as they did in New York.

At this stage, Dwight's loyalty to the mafia is still evident. He views his assignment to Tulsa as a duty rather than an exile, a test of his resilience and commitment to the family. However, his early days in Tulsa expose him to the limitations of this loyalty, as he begins to see that his years of dedication were rewarded with isolation rather than respect. This realization is the first step in his character growth, as Dwight slowly starts questioning his loyalty to a system that left him stranded. This stage of his journey is marked by self-doubt and reflection, with Dwight beginning to recognize that his past may not hold all the answers for his future.

The initial stage of Dwight's journey in Tulsa sets the foundation for his transformation. He starts to see himself as more than a mere mobster; he is a man with the potential to build something entirely new. His interactions with locals who respect him not out of fear but out of genuine admiration for his character provide him with a different kind of fulfillment, sowing the seeds for his eventual redefinition of loyalty and leadership.

Building Relationships: Loyalty Beyond the Mafia

As Dwight's influence grows, so does his network of allies. Figures like Bodhi, the cautious bar owner; Mitch, the loyal mechanic; and Tina, the young dealer, each play a role in his transformation. These relationships force Dwight to reassess his values and adapt his understanding of loyalty. Unlike his past in New York, where loyalty was enforced through fear and tradition, Tulsa offers Dwight the chance to cultivate loyalty based on respect and trust.

Dwight's relationship with Bodhi is particularly significant, as it marks a shift from authority-based loyalty to partnership. Bodhi's initial reluctance to work with Dwight gradually gives way to respect as Dwight proves his commitment to their alliance. This partnership allows Dwight to see the value of collaboration, as he realizes that true loyalty is born from mutual respect rather than fear. By valuing Bodhi's independence and expertise, Dwight fosters a loyalty that feels genuine, marking a significant departure from the hierarchical loyalty he experienced in New York.

Similarly, Dwight's interactions with Mitch reveal his capacity for mentorship and guidance, a role he has never fully embraced before. As Mitch becomes one of Dwight's most trusted allies, Dwight learns that leadership is not about enforcing control but empowering others to take ownership of their roles. Through these relationships, Dwight begins to redefine his understanding of loyalty, recognizing that it can be built on equality and mutual benefit rather than hierarchy and coercion. This shift in perspective is a key moment in Dwight's character growth, as he starts to view his allies not as subordinates but as partners in a shared vision.

Adapting to Modern Challenges: The Technology Gap

One of the recurring challenges Dwight faces in Tulsa is adapting to the world of modern technology, a struggle that reflects his need to let go of the past and embrace new ways of thinking. From his initial confusion with smartphones and social media to his skepticism about digital payment systems, Dwight's technological adaptation is both humorous and symbolic of his broader transformation. Each new piece of technology he learns represents a step toward accepting the changing world around him and a willingness to adapt rather than cling to outdated methods.

This journey with technology forces Dwight to confront his own limitations, a humbling experience that gradually chips away at his sense of invincibility. By relying on figures like Bodhi and Tina to help him navigate the digital world, Dwight learns to delegate and to trust others in areas where he lacks expertise. This shift in mindset allows Dwight to expand his network and enhance his influence, showing that true strength lies in adaptability and collaboration.

The technological challenges Dwight faces also serve as a metaphor for his transition from an old-school mobster to a modern-day leader. His willingness to embrace new tools and methods reflects his openness to growth, proving that he is capable of change despite his deeply ingrained habits. This adaptability becomes one of Dwight's defining traits, showing that he is not just a relic of the past but a man with the resilience to evolve and thrive in a new world.

Confronting Betrayal and Redefining Trust

As Dwight's empire expands, he faces moments of betrayal that force him to confront the limits of loyalty and trust. These betrayals, whether from rivals like Red or even those within his own network, serve as painful reminders of the reality of the criminal underworld, where allegiance is often fleeting and self-interest reigns supreme. Each act of betrayal is a test of Dwight's character, compelling him to reevaluate whom he can trust and how he can foster a network that values loyalty as much as he does.

Rather than reacting impulsively, Dwight approaches betrayal with a level of pragmatism and restraint that reflects his growth. Instead of resorting to immediate retribution, he carefully assesses each situation, weighing the potential impact of his response on his network's stability. This shift from reactionary violence to strategic decision-making reveals Dwight's maturation as a leader, showing that he values long-term relationships over temporary displays of power.

These experiences with betrayal also force Dwight to redefine trust, moving away from blind allegiance toward trust built on shared values and mutual respect. Through these moments of conflict, Dwight learns that true loyalty cannot be enforced; it must be earned and nurtured. This lesson marks a turning point in his character growth, as he realizes that building a lasting empire requires loyalty that is freely given, not demanded.

Developing a Sense of Responsibility: The Mentor and Protector

As Dwight's network in Tulsa grows, he takes on a mentor role that adds a new dimension to his character. Figures like Tina and Mitch look up to him not just as a leader but as a source of guidance, wisdom, and protection. This paternal role is a departure from Dwight's past, where he operated as a soldier and capo with little focus on nurturing others. In Tulsa, however, he becomes a mentor who imparts lessons, offers protection, and provides direction to those around him.

This shift reflects Dwight's evolving sense of responsibility. Rather than viewing his allies as tools for achieving his goals, he begins to see them as individuals who rely on him for support and guidance. His willingness to protect them, even at personal risk, demonstrates his commitment to creating a community where loyalty is reciprocal and trust is earned. Through this role, Dwight finds a sense of fulfillment that goes beyond power or profit, as he begins to see his legacy not in terms of control but in the positive impact he has on those around him.

Dwight's role as a mentor also allows him to make amends for his past, offering him a chance to guide others away from the mistakes he once made. By teaching his allies the values that have shaped his own life, he finds a form of redemption, showing that true power lies not in domination but in the ability to uplift and empower others. This evolution reflects Stallone's portrayal of Dwight as a character who grows through his relationships, finding a sense of purpose that transcends the material gains of the criminal world.

Wrestling with Morality and Personal Redemption

One of the most significant aspects of Dwight's growth is his journey toward personal redemption. While he initially arrives in Tulsa with a focus on reestablishing his power, he gradually begins to question the morality of his choices and the impact of his actions on those around him. This moral introspection is a departure from his past in New York, where his loyalty to the mafia left little room for self-reflection or ethical dilemmas. In Tulsa, however, Dwight is faced with choices that force him to confront his own values and question what kind of legacy he wants to leave behind.

Through moments of self-reflection, Dwight comes to understand that redemption is not about erasing his past but about creating a future that reflects his growth. His decisions become more measured and considerate, as he strives to build an empire that operates with a level of integrity and honor. This shift in mindset is a testament to his character growth, showing that he is not just a man defined by his past mistakes but someone who actively seeks to make amends and create something meaningful.

This journey toward redemption is also marked by Dwight's increasing willingness to confront his own vulnerability. While he begins the series as a seemingly invincible figure, his experiences in Tulsa reveal a more human side, a man who is not immune to regret, guilt, or the desire for peace. By embracing these vulnerabilities, Dwight finds strength in self-awareness, proving that true growth comes from the courage to face one's flaws and strive for something better.

The Search for Legacy: A New Definition of Success

As the series progresses, Dwight's goals shift from merely reestablishing his power to creating a legacy that reflects his values. He comes to see that true success is not measured by wealth or influence but by the loyalty, respect, and unity he fosters within his network. This shift is significant, as it marks Dwight's transition from a man seeking power to a leader who understands that a lasting legacy is built on trust, compassion, and shared purpose.

Dwight's desire to create a legacy is evident in his dedication to building a network that values loyalty, respect, and honor. He no longer seeks to replicate the hierarchical structure of New York's mafia; instead, he strives to create a community that feels more like a family, bound by genuine loyalty rather than fear. This new definition of success reflects his growth as a leader, showing that he values the quality of his relationships over the scale of his empire.

Through this journey, Dwight finds a sense of fulfillment that goes beyond the material; he is creating a legacy that will endure, one that reflects the values he has come to cherish. This transformation is the culmination of his character growth, a testament to his resilience, adaptability, and the power of personal redemption. By the end of the series, Dwight is no longer defined by his past; he is a man who has found peace in his purpose, proving that true success lies not in power but in the impact we have on the lives of others.

Conclusion: The Evolution of Dwight "The General" Manfredi

In *Tulsa King*, Dwight Manfredi's character arc is a journey of growth, redemption, and transformation, a testament to Stallone's ability to portray a man who is as complex as he is resilient. From his early days in Tulsa, where he grapples with his loyalty to the mafia, to his role as a mentor and leader who values trust and integrity, Dwight's development is marked by moments of self-discovery and personal growth.

Through his experiences with betrayal, adaptation, and responsibility, Dwight evolves from a hardened mobster into a leader who understands the true meaning of loyalty, honor, and legacy. His journey is not just about building an empire but about finding a sense of purpose that transcends the criminal world, a legacy that reflects his growth and the positive impact he has on those around him. By the end of the series, Dwight is a character who has not only adapted to his new environment but who has transformed into a man of vision, compassion, and strength, a leader who proves that even in the harshest of worlds, there is room for redemption and growth.

In *Tulsa King*, Dwight's evolution is a testament to the power of resilience, adaptability, and the courage to redefine one's life. Through his journey, Stallone delivers a performance that resonates deeply with viewers, reminding us that even the most seasoned individuals can find new ways to grow, lead, and inspire. Dwight's transformation from mobster to mentor, from enforcer to protector, is a reflection of the human capacity for change, proving that true strength lies not in power but in the willingness to evolve and embrace a better version of oneself.

Chapter 18: The Unlikely Allies
Introduction: Strength in Unforeseen Partnerships

In *Tulsa King*, Dwight "The General" Manfredi's journey to establish his criminal empire in Tulsa is not one he undertakes alone. Far from his familiar network in New York, Dwight finds himself forced to build alliances from scratch, relying on an eclectic mix of individuals with backgrounds and values vastly different from his own. These unlikely allies—each with unique skills, perspectives, and motivations—help Dwight navigate Tulsa's complex underworld, ultimately shaping both his empire and his approach to leadership.

These alliances not only provide Dwight with essential resources and support but also challenge him to rethink his values and strategies, teaching him that true strength lies in collaboration and adaptability. From a cautious local bar owner to a principled law enforcement officer, Dwight's alliances reflect his adaptability and willingness to embrace Tulsa's diverse culture, building an empire rooted not in fear but in mutual respect and trust. This chapter delves into the key alliances Dwight forms, exploring how each partnership influences his growth, expands his influence, and adds complexity to his criminal operation.

Bodhi: The Cautious Bar Owner Turned Trusted Confidant

One of Dwight's earliest and most significant alliances is with Bodhi, the owner of a local bar. Initially, Bodhi is cautious, hesitant to engage with Dwight's criminal activities, and wary of the risks associated with aligning himself with a figure from the underworld. However, Dwight sees potential in Bodhi, recognizing his knowledge of the local scene and his established relationships within the community. Dwight's approach with Bodhi is gentle but firm; he respects Bodhi's boundaries but makes it clear that a partnership would benefit them both.

As their relationship develops, Bodhi becomes more than just a business partner; he transforms into a trusted confidant and advisor, someone Dwight can rely on for honest feedback and insight into the local landscape. Bodhi's cautious nature balances Dwight's assertiveness, offering a level-headed perspective that often tempers Dwight's decisions.

Through Bodhi, Dwight learns the importance of local knowledge and patience, two qualities that prove invaluable in building a sustainable network in Tulsa.

Bodhi's alliance also teaches Dwight the value of loyalty born from respect rather than fear. Dwight's willingness to treat Bodhi as an equal fosters a sense of loyalty that is genuine, marking a departure from the fear-driven loyalty Dwight experienced in New York. This relationship underscores a significant aspect of Dwight's growth as a leader; he begins to see that alliances built on mutual respect are more stable and fulfilling than those forged through intimidation. Through Bodhi, Dwight gains a foothold in Tulsa's social landscape, creating a foundation of trust and reliability that strengthens his empire.

Mitch: The Mechanic with a Strong Sense of Loyalty

Mitch, a skilled mechanic with connections throughout Tulsa, becomes another pivotal ally in Dwight's journey. Unlike Bodhi, Mitch is more familiar with the gray areas of Tulsa's underworld, having experience with small-scale crime and a network that includes transporters, smugglers, and those on the fringes of legality. Mitch's practical knowledge and logistical skills make him an ideal partner for Dwight, providing essential support for moving goods and expanding his influence discreetly.

Mitch's role as a logistical backbone allows Dwight to maintain a level of discretion in his operations, avoiding the attention of both rival factions and law enforcement. Mitch is more than just a functional ally; he becomes a loyal friend, someone who shares Dwight's respect for honor and loyalty. Mitch's experience with the mechanics of underground operations proves invaluable, offering Dwight insights into the complexities of Tulsa's criminal landscape that he could not have accessed otherwise.

Through his relationship with Mitch, Dwight also begins to understand the importance of offering guidance and mentorship. Mitch looks up to Dwight, valuing his wisdom and experience, and Dwight steps into this mentor role naturally, teaching Mitch the principles that have shaped his own life. This alliance is significant not only for its logistical benefits but also for the bond of loyalty it creates. Mitch's unwavering commitment to Dwight's vision strengthens Dwight's resolve, teaching him that true allies are those who believe in the purpose behind the empire, not just the profit it brings.

Tina: The Ambitious Dealer with a Desire to Prove Herself

Tina, a young and ambitious dealer in Tulsa, brings a different dynamic to Dwight's network. Eager to make a name for herself, Tina is initially wary of Dwight's old-school methods but is drawn to his strength, experience, and unwavering sense of purpose. Tina's drive and ambition resonate with Dwight, reminding him of his own early days in organized crime, and he quickly sees her potential as a powerful ally. By taking Tina under his wing, Dwight not only gains a skilled operator but also finds an opportunity to shape a younger generation of criminals with a sense of honor and integrity.

Dwight's relationship with Tina is one of mentorship and guidance, as he teaches her the importance of loyalty, respect, and strategic thinking. Through Tina, Dwight learns that influence extends beyond immediate gain; by empowering her to take control of her own path, he instills in her the values that he holds dear. This alliance provides Dwight with a sense of purpose beyond power and profit, offering him a way to leave a positive impact on Tulsa's underworld.

Tina's alliance also introduces Dwight to Tulsa's younger, more ambitious criminal circles, expanding his influence and allowing him to access new markets and opportunities. Her connections and insights into the local scene provide Dwight with valuable information, enabling him to adapt his operations to fit Tulsa's unique culture. Tina's presence in Dwight's network highlights his adaptability, showing that he is willing to embrace new ideas and perspectives to strengthen his empire.

Stacy: The Reluctant Law Enforcement Officer with a Complex Morality

One of the most unlikely and complicated alliances Dwight forms is with Stacy, a local law enforcement officer who becomes increasingly aware of his activities in Tulsa. Initially, Stacy views Dwight with suspicion, seeing him as a threat to Tulsa's peace and stability. However, as she observes his actions, she begins to see that his presence brings a certain order to the chaos of the criminal underworld. This realization creates a reluctant alliance between the two, marked by mutual respect and an understanding that they share similar goals, albeit for different reasons.

Stacy's relationship with Dwight is defined by a delicate balance of scrutiny and acceptance. She does not condone his criminal activities, but she recognizes that his influence keeps more volatile elements in check. This alliance forces Dwight to tread carefully, as he knows that any misstep could jeopardize their fragile understanding. Through Stacy, Dwight learns to navigate the gray area between law and crime, adopting a more cautious and diplomatic approach to his operations.

This alliance with Stacy adds depth to Dwight's character, showing that he is capable of earning respect even from those who are sworn to oppose him. It forces him to consider the broader impact of his actions on the community, encouraging him to adopt a more principled approach. Stacy's alliance also reflects Dwight's ability to bridge seemingly insurmountable divides, creating a network that transcends traditional boundaries and operates within a framework of mutual respect.

Red: The Rival Biker Leader and Complex Adversary

While Red, the leader of a local biker gang, is initially one of Dwight's primary antagonists, their relationship evolves into a complex alliance based on respect and mutual benefit. Red's gang controls a portion of Tulsa's drug trade, and Dwight's arrival threatens his influence, leading to a series of confrontations that test both men's resolve. However, Dwight's strategic approach and willingness to avoid unnecessary conflict gradually earn Red's begrudging respect, setting the stage for an uneasy alliance.

This alliance with Red is built on pragmatism rather than friendship. Both men recognize that they stand to gain more by working together than by clashing, and they negotiate a territorial arrangement that allows each to operate without interference. This arrangement teaches Dwight the value of diplomacy, showing him that alliances can be forged even with those who were once adversaries. Through Red, Dwight learns to navigate the complexities of rivalries, finding ways to balance power without resorting to violence.

Red's alliance also serves as a reminder of the volatility of Tulsa's criminal landscape. Unlike Dwight's other allies, Red remains a potential threat, a figure who could turn against him if the circumstances change. This tension adds a layer of suspense to their interactions, forcing Dwight to remain vigilant and strategic. Red's presence in Dwight's network highlights the delicate nature of alliances in the underworld, where loyalty is often conditional and power must be carefully balanced.

Bodhi's Connections to Tulsa's Underground Scene

Bodhi's bar is more than just a business; it becomes a central hub for Dwight's operations, a place where he can gather information, meet with allies, and observe Tulsa's underground scene. Through Bodhi, Dwight gains access to Tulsa's nightlife and social circles, connecting with individuals who operate in the gray areas of legality. Bodhi's connections provide Dwight with valuable insights into the city's pulse, allowing him to stay informed about potential threats and opportunities.

This alliance with Bodhi's network underscores the importance of community in Dwight's operation. Rather than isolating himself from Tulsa's social fabric, Dwight integrates himself into the local scene, using Bodhi's bar as a base for his interactions. This approach reflects his adaptability, as he learns to operate within Tulsa's unique culture rather than imposing his own methods. By embracing the connections Bodhi offers, Dwight expands his influence organically, creating a network that is deeply rooted in Tulsa's community.

Bodhi's bar also becomes a symbol of Dwight's impact on Tulsa. Through this alliance, Dwight not only gains a foothold in the city but also creates a space where his values of loyalty, respect, and mutual benefit are evident. This partnership with Bodhi and his connections allows Dwight to build a network that reflects his growth, showing that his influence extends beyond the criminal world and into the heart of Tulsa's social fabric.

The Community Alliance: Establishing a Broader Network of Support

As Dwight's influence in Tulsa grows, he begins to form alliances beyond the criminal underworld, connecting with local business owners, community leaders, and everyday residents. These alliances allow Dwight to position himself as a benefactor within the community, someone who supports local businesses, helps those in need, and fosters a sense of stability. By integrating himself into the community, Dwight creates a support network that extends beyond his immediate allies, giving him a broader base of influence and protection.

This alliance with the community adds a new dimension to Dwight's character, showing that he values more than just power or profit. He sees his role in Tulsa as an opportunity to make a positive impact, using his influence to create a sense of order and stability that benefits everyone. Through his interactions with the community, Dwight learns that true strength lies in the support of those around him, and he becomes increasingly invested in the well-being of Tulsa's residents.

The community's support also serves as a shield, providing Dwight with a level of protection that rivals and law enforcement find difficult to penetrate. By positioning himself as a respected figure within the community, Dwight gains a measure of legitimacy, making it harder for adversaries to turn the city against him. This broader alliance reflects his growth as a leader, showing that he understands the importance of building an empire that is not only feared but respected and valued by the people it affects.

Conclusion: The Power of Unlikely Alliances in Shaping an Empire

In *Tulsa King*, Dwight Manfredi's unlikely alliances are more than strategic partnerships; they are essential components of his journey, shaping both his character and the direction of his empire. From Bodhi's caution and Mitch's loyalty to Tina's ambition and Stacy's complex morality, each ally offers Dwight new perspectives, skills, and challenges that deepen his understanding of leadership and loyalty. These alliances reflect Dwight's adaptability, showing that he is willing to embrace Tulsa's diverse culture and build connections that transcend traditional criminal boundaries.

Through these alliances, Dwight learns that true power lies not in control but in connection. He creates a network that values mutual respect, loyalty, and shared purpose, transforming Tulsa's underworld into a community rooted in his principles. Each alliance challenges Dwight to rethink his values, teaching him that loyalty is earned, trust is mutual, and influence is most effective when it is backed by respect.

By the end of the series, Dwight's alliances have become the foundation of his empire, a testament to his growth as a leader who values relationships over domination. His unlikely allies are not just partners in crime; they are reflections of his journey, symbols of his ability to evolve and adapt in a world that is as complex as it is dangerous. Through these alliances, Dwight finds a sense of fulfillment and purpose, proving that even in the harshest of worlds, true power comes from the strength of those who stand beside you.

Chapter 19: Cliffhangers and Twists
Introduction: The Art of Suspense and Surprise

In *Tulsa King*, suspense is an essential element that keeps viewers eagerly awaiting each new episode. From unexpected betrayals and high-stakes confrontations to subtle clues that hint at deeper secrets, the series expertly weaves cliffhangers and plot twists into its narrative, creating a sense of constant tension and anticipation. These narrative devices serve more than just to shock; they reveal new facets of characters, redefine relationships, and keep the stakes perpetually high as Dwight "The General" Manfredi navigates the complexities of Tulsa's criminal underworld.

The show's ability to balance unexpected twists with carefully built suspense is a testament to its writing, which leverages Dwight's journey to create moments that are both surprising and meaningful. Each cliffhanger feels earned, adding depth to the storyline while reinforcing the themes of loyalty, betrayal, and survival that define *Tulsa King*. In this chapter, we will explore how the series crafts its most memorable twists and cliffhangers, examining the techniques used to keep viewers hooked and invested in Dwight's ever-evolving story.

The First Major Twist: Dwight's Exile to Tulsa

The first twist that hooks viewers is Dwight's unexpected exile to Tulsa, a move that comes as a surprise to both him and the audience. For a former New York mafia capo, being sent to a small, unfamiliar town feels like a demotion, a punishment rather than a reward for his years of loyalty. This twist sets the stage for the series, introducing a fish-out-of-water element that challenges Dwight to adapt to a world far removed from the organized crime landscape of New York.

Dwight's sudden relocation to Tulsa establishes an undercurrent of mystery and tension, as viewers question the motives behind his exile and whether there's a hidden agenda at play. This early twist creates a sense of unease, making it clear that Dwight is no longer in control of his fate and forcing him to operate in a place where he has no allies or established network. The shock of this twist draws viewers in, sparking curiosity about how Dwight will adjust to this new environment and whether he will be able to regain the power and influence he once held.

This twist also raises questions about Dwight's relationship with the mafia family he served, hinting at possible betrayal or abandonment by those he once trusted. By setting the stage with this unexpected shift, *Tulsa King* establishes a tone of uncertainty that lingers throughout the series, making viewers question not only Dwight's future but also the reliability of the alliances he forms along the way.

Betrayals and Shifting Loyalties: Cliffhangers That Redefine Relationships

One of the most effective ways *Tulsa King* keeps viewers engaged is through cliffhangers that reveal betrayals and shifts in loyalty. These moments of betrayal are not only shocking but also serve to deepen the emotional stakes, as Dwight is forced to confront the reality that trust is a rare and fragile commodity in Tulsa's underworld. Each betrayal is carefully foreshadowed, with subtle hints that build suspense before the reveal, creating a sense of dread that keeps viewers on edge.

A notable example of this is the cliffhanger involving an ally who secretly works against Dwight, leaking information to a rival in exchange for personal gain. When Dwight discovers this betrayal, the suspense reaches a peak, as viewers are left wondering how he will respond and what impact this disloyalty will have on his network. The reveal adds complexity to the story, forcing Dwight to rethink his trust in those around him and reevaluate his approach to leadership. By ending episodes with these revelations, the series keeps viewers invested, eager to see how Dwight will navigate the shifting landscape of loyalty.

These betrayals also highlight Dwight's vulnerability, reminding viewers that even a seasoned mobster can be caught off guard. The unpredictability of these moments serves as a powerful narrative tool, as it makes clear that no alliance is immune to fracture. This continuous reshuffling of loyalties injects suspense into each episode, as viewers are never quite certain who will stand by Dwight and who will ultimately betray him.

High-Stakes Confrontations and Narrow Escapes

Another key element of *Tulsa King*'s suspenseful storytelling is its high-stakes confrontations, many of which end in cliffhangers that leave Dwight's fate uncertain. These moments are carefully crafted, building tension through escalating conflicts that reach their climax at just the right moment. Each confrontation adds layers to the story, revealing Dwight's strategic mind and resilience while keeping viewers on edge as he navigates life-or-death situations.

One memorable cliffhanger involves a standoff between Dwight and Red, the leader of a biker gang, where tensions reach a boiling point. The scene is built up with a slow, deliberate pacing, as both men engage in a battle of wills that leaves viewers anticipating a violent clash. Just when it seems like a resolution is within reach, the episode cuts to black, leaving viewers unsure of how the encounter will end. This cliffhanger heightens the suspense, compelling viewers to tune in to the next episode to see how Dwight handles the threat and whether his tactical approach will prove successful.

These close calls and narrow escapes serve to humanize Dwight, showing that despite his experience and cunning, he is not invulnerable. The show balances his strategic brilliance with moments of vulnerability, keeping viewers invested in his survival. By crafting these intense encounters, *Tulsa King* creates a series of mini-cliffhangers that sustain the tension, making each episode feel like a chapter in an unfolding story where the outcome is never certain.

Unexpected Twists in Dwight's Personal Journey

In addition to the suspense surrounding Dwight's criminal empire, *Tulsa King* incorporates twists related to Dwight's personal journey, adding emotional depth to the series. As Dwight adapts to life in Tulsa, he encounters people and situations that challenge his understanding of loyalty, family, and redemption. These twists reveal new layers to his character, showing that his journey is as much about self-discovery as it is about building an empire.

One such twist involves a sudden reappearance of someone from Dwight's past, forcing him to confront unresolved issues and question the choices he has made. This encounter introduces a new dimension to Dwight's character, revealing vulnerabilities and regrets that he has long kept buried. The unexpected nature of this twist catches both Dwight and the audience off guard, providing a moment of introspection that adds complexity to his character arc. By intertwining personal revelations with the main plot, *Tulsa King* keeps viewers invested not only in Dwight's external conflicts but also in his inner journey.

These personal twists also serve as a reminder that Dwight's life is not defined solely by his criminal activities; he is a man searching for meaning, legacy, and perhaps even redemption. Each revelation brings him closer to understanding himself, creating a sense of narrative continuity that makes every twist feel purposeful. By ending episodes with these personal cliffhangers, the show keeps viewers engaged on multiple levels, making them invested in both the man and the empire he is building.

Red Herrings and Misdirection: Keeping Viewers Guessing

Tulsa King also employs red herrings and misdirection to keep viewers guessing, using subtle hints and misleading clues to create suspense. By introducing plot elements that appear significant but ultimately lead in unexpected directions, the series builds anticipation and surprise, subverting expectations in ways that feel organic to the story. These red herrings create an atmosphere of unpredictability, as viewers are never quite sure which clues will be important and which will lead them astray.

One effective use of misdirection involves an apparent betrayal that turns out to be a misunderstanding, throwing Dwight and his allies into turmoil. The episode builds tension around this perceived betrayal, with viewers anticipating a dramatic fallout, only for the reveal to show that the situation was more complex than it initially appeared. This twist not only surprises the audience but also strengthens the bonds within Dwight's network, showing that loyalty can be tested but still remain intact. These moments of misdirection add depth to the narrative, making viewers question every alliance and keeping them engaged in the story's nuances.

This use of red herrings also extends to Dwight's interactions with law enforcement, where certain clues and behaviors suggest that his operation is close to being exposed. By creating a sense of impending danger that occasionally proves to be false, the show sustains tension without sacrificing believability. These moments keep viewers on edge, as they constantly anticipate a twist that could change everything. The unpredictability of these red herrings adds a layer of psychological suspense, making each episode feel like a puzzle that viewers are eager to solve.

The Season Finale Cliffhanger: Setting the Stage for Future Conflicts

Tulsa King concludes its season with a dramatic cliffhanger that leaves viewers eagerly awaiting the next chapter in Dwight's journey. This final twist not only raises the stakes but also introduces new challenges, allies, and potential enemies, setting the stage for a continuation of Dwight's story. The season finale cliffhanger serves as the culmination of the series' various plotlines, drawing together loose ends while introducing fresh mysteries that promise to deepen the intrigue.

In the season finale, Dwight finds himself facing a seemingly insurmountable threat that could dismantle everything he has built. The episode builds suspense as he tries to outmaneuver his adversaries, only to end with a revelation that changes the course of his journey. This twist redefines the stakes, reminding viewers that Dwight's empire is far from secure and that the challenges ahead will be even more formidable. By ending the season on a note of uncertainty, *Tulsa King* keeps viewers invested in Dwight's future, sparking speculation and anticipation for what lies ahead.

This season-ending cliffhanger also serves to reinforce the series' themes of loyalty, betrayal, and resilience. Dwight's response to this final twist highlights his growth as a leader and his commitment to his network, setting the stage for new alliances and rivalries in the next season. By leaving Dwight's fate uncertain, the show creates a sense of continuity, making it clear that his journey is far from over. This cliffhanger is both satisfying and tantalizing, providing enough closure to conclude the season while leaving viewers eager to see how Dwight will navigate the challenges to come.

Conclusion: The Power of Cliffhangers and Twists in *Tulsa King*

In *Tulsa King*, cliffhangers and plot twists are not merely narrative devices; they are essential to the show's storytelling, adding layers of suspense, surprise, and emotional depth to Dwight Manfredi's journey. From unexpected betrayals and high-stakes confrontations to personal revelations and red herrings, each twist keeps viewers engaged, invested, and eager to see what happens next. The series skillfully balances these elements, ensuring that each cliffhanger feels purposeful and connected to the broader narrative, adding complexity to both the characters and the story.

The show's ability to weave these twists into Dwight's personal and professional life is a testament to its writing, which understands that suspense is most effective when it serves a deeper purpose. Each cliffhanger reveals something new about Dwight, forcing him to confront his vulnerabilities, question his loyalties, and adapt to an ever-changing world. By keeping viewers guessing, *Tulsa King* creates a sense of unpredictability that mirrors Dwight's own journey, making the series a compelling exploration of resilience, ambition, and the complexities of human relationships.

Ultimately, the twists and cliffhangers in *Tulsa King* are a reflection of Dwight's world, where nothing is certain and every decision carries risk. Through these moments of suspense, the series not only keeps viewers hooked but also deepens their connection to Dwight's story, proving that great storytelling lies not just in the destination but in the journey. As viewers navigate the twists and turns alongside Dwight, they become part of a world where loyalty is tested, alliances are forged and broken, and the future is as unpredictable as the people who shape it.

Chapter 20: What's Next for *Tulsa King*?
Introduction: The Excitement and Speculation Ahead

As *Tulsa King* closes its first season with a cliffhanger that leaves viewers eagerly anticipating the next chapter, fans are left speculating on the future of Dwight "The General" Manfredi and the world he's building in Tulsa. The series has crafted a rich, complex narrative that combines intense action with character-driven storytelling, making the stakes higher with each episode. Given the plot twists, betrayals, and alliances of the first season, there's no doubt that the story will only deepen as Dwight faces new threats, builds more connections, and wrestles with his ambitions and loyalties.

In this chapter, we explore the possible directions the show might take in its next season, offering speculation on Dwight's journey, emerging rivalries, evolving relationships, and new themes that might come to the forefront. From potential alliances to deepening personal conflicts, the next season of *Tulsa King* promises to elevate Dwight's story, testing his resolve, challenging his values, and expanding his influence in ways that will keep fans eagerly tuned in.

1. The Threat from New York: A Return of the Mafia's Influence

One of the most likely storylines to emerge in the upcoming season is a renewed threat from Dwight's former mafia family in New York. With Dwight's successful establishment of a criminal network in Tulsa, his independence has become more apparent, which could be seen as a challenge—or even a betrayal—by the New York syndicate. The idea that Dwight's old bosses might see him as a rogue player who needs to be reined in opens the door to intense conflict and potential violence.

The arrival of emissaries or enforcers from New York would introduce a new level of tension and danger, forcing Dwight to navigate the fine line between staying true to his principles and defending his new empire. This conflict could also bring up unresolved issues from Dwight's past, forcing him to confront former loyalties and question his allegiance to the mafia that exiled him. Dwight's response to the pressure from New York will reveal how far he's come and how much he values the community he has built in Tulsa.

Additionally, the threat from New York may lead Dwight to make strategic alliances with local rivals and figures in Tulsa to solidify his base and fend off any attempts to regain control over him. This storyline would provide high-stakes drama, as Dwight's network faces off against the experienced, well-resourced power of the mafia, pushing him to make tough decisions that could ultimately determine the future of his empire.

2. New Allies and Rivalries in Tulsa's Underworld

While Dwight has built a loyal network in Tulsa, his continued success and rising influence will inevitably attract attention from other local criminal factions. The next season could introduce new characters from Tulsa's criminal underworld, each with their own motives, skills, and ambitions. Some may see Dwight's operation as an opportunity for profit, while others may view him as a threat to their own power. These new alliances and rivalries will force Dwight to navigate a more complex and potentially volatile criminal landscape, adding layers to his journey.

Potential new rivals could include local crime families, biker gangs from neighboring regions, or even corrupt businesspeople who wish to tap into Dwight's resources. These new players would add a fresh level of tension, as Dwight balances alliances with potential adversaries who may turn on him when it's convenient. Each new alliance or rivalry has the potential to shake up Dwight's network, putting his leadership skills to the test as he figures out whom he can trust and who is only in it for their own gain.

New allies might bring valuable resources, insight, or manpower that would help Dwight defend his empire from external threats, especially as the stakes get higher with New York's looming presence. These alliances could introduce characters who add unique dynamics to the storyline, offering Dwight not only new resources but also challenging him to adapt to the evolving criminal landscape in Tulsa. This expansion of

Tulsa's criminal world will give the show even more room to explore themes of loyalty, ambition, and betrayal, enhancing the show's suspense and complexity.

3. Internal Struggles and Leadership Challenges

As Dwight's network grows, so will the challenges of maintaining loyalty and order among his allies. The next season could explore the pressures Dwight faces in balancing the diverse personalities and motivations within his organization, as he juggles the conflicting interests and expectations of figures like Bodhi, Mitch, and Tina. These internal struggles are likely to escalate as Dwight's operation expands, forcing him to make tough decisions that will test his leadership and possibly even create rifts among his closest allies.

For instance, Bodhi's cautious approach may clash with the more ambitious attitudes of younger players like Tina, leading to internal conflict that Dwight must mediate. Mitch, who has always been loyal, may also find himself questioning Dwight's choices if they put the entire operation at risk, adding an element of tension and emotional depth to the story. These leadership challenges will reveal Dwight's growth as a leader, showcasing his ability to adapt to the demands of a larger, more complex organization. However, they may also expose his vulnerabilities, making him more human and relatable as he struggles to keep his allies united.

As Dwight navigates these internal challenges, he may be forced to confront questions of loyalty and trust, testing the strength of the bonds he has built. These moments of internal struggle could offer viewers insight into Dwight's character, revealing his commitment to those he leads and the sacrifices he is willing to make to protect them. By exploring these dynamics, the next season will add depth to Dwight's story, showing that the real challenges of leadership often come not from external threats but from the people we trust the most.

4. The Evolution of Dwight's Relationship with Stacy

One of the most intriguing dynamics in *Tulsa King* is Dwight's relationship with Stacy, the local law enforcement officer who has become aware of his influence in Tulsa. The next season could see this relationship evolve in unexpected ways, as Stacy grapples with her duty to uphold the law while acknowledging the stability Dwight brings to the city's criminal landscape. This complex relationship could take on new dimensions, as both Stacy and Dwight begin to see each other not as enemies but as reluctant allies.

Stacy's internal conflict may intensify as she becomes further entangled with Dwight's world, facing ethical dilemmas that challenge her sense of duty. She may find herself questioning whether allowing Dwight's presence in Tulsa is ultimately beneficial, as his influence keeps the more dangerous elements of Tulsa's underworld in check. This moral ambiguity could lead Stacy to make compromises, forcing her to walk a tightrope between her professional obligations and her understanding of what is best for the community.

This storyline could also introduce personal tension between Stacy and Dwight, as they develop a begrudging respect for each other's principles and goals. The evolution of their relationship could offer insight into both characters, revealing their vulnerabilities, values, and shared sense of justice. By exploring this dynamic, the next season could add a layer of emotional depth to the show, showing that the line between law and crime is often blurred, especially when both sides are driven by a desire to protect the people around them.

5. Dwight's Quest for Legacy and Redemption

Dwight's journey in *Tulsa King* is not just about building an empire; it's also about finding a sense of purpose and legacy. In the upcoming season, we may see Dwight grappling more deeply with questions of redemption and the legacy he wishes to leave behind. Having endured betrayal, isolation, and exile, Dwight's experiences in Tulsa offer him a chance to build something meaningful—a network that values loyalty, respect, and mutual benefit over the rigid hierarchies and betrayal he experienced in New York.

This quest for legacy could lead Dwight to make decisions that prioritize his principles over profit, creating moments of self-reflection and growth that deepen his character. As he faces threats from New York and pressures within his network, Dwight may be forced to confront the moral compromises he has made along the way, questioning whether his actions align with the values he claims to hold. This introspection could add a philosophical element to the story, exploring themes of redemption, honor, and the search for meaning in a world defined by violence and power.

Dwight's desire for legacy may also influence his relationships with his allies, particularly figures like Tina, whom he views as a protégé. By mentoring the next generation, Dwight has the opportunity to create a legacy that extends beyond his lifetime, leaving behind an empire that reflects his values. This pursuit of legacy offers a compelling contrast to the typical mobster narrative, showing that Dwight is not just building an empire for himself but is seeking a form of redemption that transcends his past.

6. Expanding Tulsa's Criminal Landscape and New Enemies

The next season is likely to explore the broader criminal landscape surrounding Tulsa, introducing new enemies and challenges from outside the city. With Dwight's growing influence, his empire may attract the attention of criminal organizations from neighboring regions, such as biker gangs, cartels, or other powerful figures who see Tulsa as a potential expansion zone. These new enemies will raise the stakes, forcing Dwight to adapt his strategies and defend his territory against forces that may be more ruthless and well-resourced than those he has encountered so far.

These external threats could introduce high-stakes action sequences and plot twists, pushing Dwight to his limits as he fights to protect his empire. The arrival of new enemies will also challenge his alliances, as he may need to rally his network and even forge temporary partnerships with former rivals to fend off a common threat. This expansion of Tulsa's criminal landscape will add a new layer of complexity to the series, broadening the scope of the story and creating opportunities for unexpected alliances, betrayals, and power struggles.

This storyline also presents the opportunity to delve deeper into the socio-political dynamics of organized crime, exploring how different factions operate and the alliances they form to protect their interests. By expanding the criminal landscape, the next season can keep the series fresh, introducing new characters, conflicts, and stakes that elevate Dwight's journey and challenge him to evolve as a leader.

7. Potential Return of Key Figures from Dwight's Past

A tantalizing possibility for the next season is the return of key figures from Dwight's past, such as former allies or family members who resurface in Tulsa. These figures could bring unresolved conflicts, buried secrets, or old loyalties that challenge Dwight's commitment to his new life. The return of individuals from Dwight's past would provide an opportunity to explore his backstory, adding depth to his character and revealing the motivations and experiences that have shaped him.

For instance, a former ally from New York who arrives in Tulsa could force Dwight to confront unresolved issues or make choices that test his loyalty to his new network. These returning figures might also introduce complex emotional conflicts, as Dwight must balance his loyalty to his past with his commitment to the future he is building. This storyline would add an emotional layer to the series, showing that Dwight's journey is not just about survival but about reconciling the different parts of his identity.

The return of figures from Dwight's past could also provide insight into the trauma and sacrifices that have defined his life, revealing the personal costs of his loyalty to the mafia. By exploring these relationships, the next season can offer viewers a more nuanced understanding of Dwight's character, showing that even a man as resilient as Dwight carries emotional scars that shape his choices and values.

Conclusion: A Promising Future for *Tulsa King*

The next season of *Tulsa King* holds tremendous potential, promising to elevate Dwight Manfredi's journey with fresh conflicts, evolving relationships, and deeper explorations of legacy and redemption. From renewed threats from New York and emerging alliances within Tulsa's criminal landscape to Dwight's personal journey of self-discovery and legacy, the series has the opportunity to expand its scope while maintaining the rich character-driven storytelling that defines it.

As Dwight faces new enemies, redefines old alliances, and navigates the complexities of his criminal empire, the next season will continue to explore themes of loyalty, power, and the search for meaning in an unpredictable world. Viewers can expect more of the twists, cliffhangers, and intense drama that have made *Tulsa King* so compelling, with each episode pushing Dwight closer to his ultimate goal while revealing the sacrifices and challenges that come with building a legacy.

Ultimately, the future of *Tulsa King* is as unpredictable as the world Dwight inhabits, promising a thrilling ride for fans who have come to invest deeply in his journey. With high stakes, moral dilemmas, and the constant threat of betrayal, the next season will undoubtedly keep viewers on the edge of their seats, eager to see what's next for Dwight and the empire he's determined to protect.

Appendix

Appendix A: A Guide to the Cast and Characters

Tulsa King boasts a diverse and dynamic cast of characters, each bringing depth and complexity to the world of Dwight "The General" Manfredi and the criminal underworld he navigates. From steadfast allies to formidable rivals, these characters contribute to the rich tapestry of relationships, conflicts, and motivations that drive the series. This guide offers a brief description of the main and supporting characters, exploring their backgrounds, motivations, and relationships with Dwight as they each play a role in shaping the series' narrative.

Main Characters

Dwight "The General" Manfredi (Sylvester Stallone)

Dwight Manfredi, known as "The General," is a seasoned mobster from New York exiled to Tulsa by his mafia family after serving a 25-year prison sentence. A natural leader with a strict personal code of honor, Dwight is both ruthless and principled, valuing loyalty and respect above all. Despite his age, Dwight's experience and strategic mind make him a formidable figure as he begins building his empire from scratch in an unfamiliar city. His journey in Tulsa is not only about establishing power but also about finding redemption, leaving behind a meaningful legacy, and redefining loyalty and leadership in a place far removed from his past.

Bodhi (Martin Starr)

Bodhi is the cautious owner of a local bar in Tulsa and one of Dwight's first allies. Initially wary of getting involved with a mobster, Bodhi gradually comes to respect Dwight's vision and determination, becoming a trusted confidant. Bodhi's cautious nature contrasts with Dwight's assertive approach, providing a voice of reason and a grounded perspective. Over time, Bodhi's bar becomes the central hub for Dwight's operations, with Bodhi playing a key role in gathering information and facilitating local connections. His alliance with Dwight challenges him to step out of his comfort zone, ultimately fostering a sense of loyalty based on mutual respect.

Mitch (Garrett Hedlund)

Mitch is a skilled mechanic with a strong sense of loyalty and a network of underground connections in Tulsa. As Dwight's logistical backbone, Mitch handles transportation, discreet transactions, and provides essential support for expanding Dwight's empire. Mitch's blue-collar sensibility and street-smart approach make him an invaluable ally, and he respects Dwight's experience and wisdom. Their friendship is marked by loyalty and mutual trust, with Mitch looking up to Dwight as a mentor and learning from his strategic insights. Mitch's steadfast loyalty underscores Dwight's ability to inspire those around him, and his dedication becomes a cornerstone of Dwight's operation in Tulsa.

Tina (Jay Will)

Tina is a young, ambitious dealer in Tulsa who sees Dwight's arrival as an opportunity to make a name for herself. Eager to prove her worth, she is drawn to Dwight's strength and charisma, viewing him as both a mentor and a father figure. Dwight, in turn, sees potential in Tina, guiding her in the ways of loyalty and strategic thinking. Tina's ambition and loyalty make her a valuable asset, helping Dwight expand his influence within Tulsa's younger criminal circles. Her presence also brings out Dwight's protective side, as he takes on a mentorship role, imparting his values to the next generation.

Stacy (Andrea Savage)

Stacy is a principled local law enforcement officer who quickly becomes aware of Dwight's presence in Tulsa. Initially viewing him as a threat, Stacy develops a complex relationship with Dwight, recognizing that his influence brings a level of order to the city's criminal underworld. Caught between her duty to uphold the law and her understanding of Dwight's impact, Stacy becomes a reluctant ally, facing ethical dilemmas that challenge her sense of justice. Her relationship with Dwight is marked by mutual respect and moral ambiguity, as she navigates the blurred lines between law and crime.

Red (Domenick Lombardozzi)

Red is the leader of a local biker gang who initially sees Dwight as a threat to his territory. Used to asserting control through intimidation, Red's confrontational approach contrasts with Dwight's strategic, calculated style. However, Dwight's resilience and willingness to negotiate gradually earn Red's grudging respect, resulting in an uneasy alliance. Red's unpredictable nature and self-interest make him a complex character, one who may work with Dwight when convenient but who remains a potential rival. His alliance with Dwight underscores the precarious nature of power in Tulsa's criminal underworld, where loyalties are conditional and alliances fragile.

Supporting Characters

Bobby (Max Casella)

Bobby is a local Tulsa resident and longtime friend of Mitch, who occasionally assists with logistical support for Dwight's network. Streetwise and resourceful, Bobby knows the ins and outs of Tulsa's underground scene, and his connections are helpful in gathering information and running smaller tasks. Though not directly involved in Dwight's operations, Bobby's local knowledge and informal connections offer a unique advantage, providing insights into rival factions and other potential threats. His pragmatic approach to survival in Tulsa's underworld adds a layer of depth to the supporting cast, making him a valuable resource for Dwight's growing empire.

Lila (Dana Delany)

Lila is the owner of a local pawn shop in Tulsa with her own history of navigating the darker corners of the city's underworld. Independent and fiercely protective of her interests, Lila initially interacts with Dwight as a business contact, offering valuable assets and supplies for his operation. Her cautious approach makes her wary of Dwight, but she eventually grows to respect his dedication and strategic mind. Lila's knowledge of Tulsa's criminal landscape provides Dwight with useful insights and connections, and her pawn shop serves as a neutral meeting ground for discussions and deals.

Vince (Vincent Piazza)

Vince is an emissary from Dwight's former mafia family in New York, sent to monitor his activities in Tulsa and assess whether he is still loyal to the family. Vince's arrival in Tulsa introduces tension, as his presence threatens to disrupt Dwight's independence and bring him back under New York's control. Though they share a history, Vince's allegiance to the New York syndicate creates a rift, making him both a reminder of Dwight's past and a symbol of the control the family still hopes to exert over him. His character adds intrigue to the series, providing a direct link to Dwight's unresolved issues with the mafia.

Jackie (Jessica Lee)

Jackie is a local business owner who befriends Dwight and offers a unique connection to Tulsa's legitimate business community. Her honest and upfront approach contrasts with the more secretive characters in Dwight's network, providing him with insights into the town's local culture and offering a bridge between his criminal world and the ordinary lives of Tulsa's residents. Jackie's friendship challenges Dwight to think about his impact on the community and question the long-term consequences of his actions. Her presence in the series adds depth to Dwight's character, showing that he is capable of forming connections outside of his criminal empire.

Ricky (E.J. Bonilla)

Ricky is a young, impulsive member of Red's biker gang who sees Dwight as both a mentor and a threat. While he admires Dwight's reputation and experience, Ricky's loyalty to Red creates tension between him and Dwight. He is ambitious and eager to prove himself, but his impulsive nature often leads him into risky situations, creating challenges for both Red and Dwight. Ricky's character reflects the struggle for power and respect within Tulsa's criminal landscape, serving as a foil for Dwight's seasoned and calculated approach to conflict.

Calvin (David Pasquesi)

Calvin is a low-level criminal with connections in Tulsa's drug trade, providing a link to the city's street-level operations. Initially a minor figure, Calvin becomes a key asset for Dwight, assisting with distribution and providing valuable information on local rivalries. Calvin's ambition makes him eager to align himself with Dwight's growing empire, but his loyalty is often tested by the more lucrative offers from rival gangs. Calvin's character reflects the volatility of Tulsa's criminal underworld, where alliances shift quickly, and loyalty is frequently conditional.

Recurring Characters
Angela (Wendie Malick)

Angela is a long-standing acquaintance of Dwight from New York, who occasionally visits Tulsa to offer advice, support, and connections back to the mafia world. While Angela is loyal to Dwight, her continued ties to the New York syndicate create a tension that complicates her relationship with him. Her character serves as a reminder of Dwight's past and the ties that still bind him, adding emotional weight to his struggle for independence.

Carlos (Frankie Faison)

Carlos is a veteran associate of the mafia who acted as a mentor to Dwight during his early days in organized crime. Although he remains in New York, Carlos keeps a watchful eye on Dwight's progress in Tulsa, occasionally sending messages or emissaries to remind Dwight of the syndicate's influence. His character provides backstory for Dwight's formative years and serves as a link to the traditional mafia values that Dwight both respects and resents.

Jimmy "Jimmy the Hammer" Benedetto (Chazz Palminteri)

Jimmy Benedetto, known as "Jimmy the Hammer," is a powerful figure in New York's mafia and one of Dwight's former allies. His involvement in Dwight's exile to Tulsa is hinted at throughout the series, and his influence looms over Dwight's operations as a constant, if indirect, threat. Jimmy's ruthless reputation and tight grip on the family make him a figure that Dwight both respects and dreads. Should Jimmy make a personal appearance in Tulsa, it could signify a shift in Dwight's journey, forcing him to confront his past head-on.

Conclusion: A Cast that Shapes the World of *Tulsa King*

The characters in *Tulsa King* bring depth and richness to the world Dwight Manfredi inhabits, each offering unique perspectives, challenges, and motivations that contribute to the series' compelling narrative. From loyal allies and formidable adversaries to moral figures and pragmatic survivors, each character reflects a different aspect of Dwight's journey, challenging him to adapt, grow, and define his place within Tulsa's criminal landscape.

Together, this diverse cast creates a tapestry of relationships that adds emotional depth and complexity to the series, making *Tulsa King* a story not only of power and ambition but of the human connections that define and shape us. As Dwight's journey continues, these characters will undoubtedly play pivotal roles in the twists, conflicts, and alliances that define the world of *Tulsa King*, leaving viewers eager to see how each individual influences the unfolding story.

Appendix B: Episode Guide
Season 1: Episode Guide

1. **Episode 1: "Go West, Old Man"** – November 13, 2022
   Dwight, blindsided by the mafia's decision to exile him to Tulsa, begins making connections to establish his new empire.
2. **Episode 2: "Center of the Universe"** – November 20, 2022
   Dwight, Bodhi, and Tyson embark on a business road trip, while Stacy investigates Dwight's background.
3. **Episode 3: "Caprice"** – November 27, 2022
   Dwight finds a new business opportunity, but a routine errand has unexpected consequences.
4. **Episode 4: "Visitation Place"** – December 4, 2022
   Dwight's crew tests a new plan at the Tulsa Arena but faces a major roadblock.
5. **Episode 5: "Token Joe"** – December 11, 2022
   Dwight returns to New York, reuniting with family, while back in Tulsa, Tyson faces his own trouble.
6. **Episode 6: "Stable"** – December 18, 2022
   Dwight visits his daughter, Tina, and confronts family issues before returning to Tulsa to make Mitch a crucial offer.
7. **Episode 7: "Warr Acres"** – December 25, 2022
   Stacy faces serious consequences for her decisions, while Dwight and Armand work together to clean up.
8. **Episode 8: "Adobe Walls"** – January 1, 2023
   Dwight's plans for a casino escalate as Stacy faces a showdown with Caolan Waltrip's biker gang.

9. **Episode 9: "Happy Trails"** – January 8, 2023
   Tensions peak as Dwight's crew faces off against Waltrip's gang in a climactic battle. A flashback sheds light on Dwight's past.

Season 2: Episode Guide

1. **Episode 1: "Back in the Saddle"** – September 15, 2024
   Dwight prepares to open his new casino and weed business but faces resistance from local law enforcement.
2. **Episode 2: "Kansas City Blues"** – September 22, 2024
   A family member from Dwight's past arrives, and the Kansas City Mob starts paying attention to his operation.
3. **Episode 3: "Oklahoma v. Manfredi"** – September 29, 2024
   Dwight faces a legal challenge in a high-stakes courtroom drama.
4. **Episode 4: "Heroes and Villains"** – October 6, 2024
   Dwight and Bodhi consider a new investment, while newcomer Thresher tests his limits.
5. **Episode 5: "Tilting at Windmills"** – October 13, 2024
   Thresher takes bold steps against Dwight's crew, with tensions growing inside the New York Mob.
6. **Episode 6: "Navigator"** – October 20, 2024
   Dwight holds meetings with representatives from Kansas City and New York, while Tyson seeks his place in the operation.
7. **Episode 7: "Life Support"** – October 27, 2024
   Dwight investigates an attack on his crew, as Stacy faces increasing challenges balancing duty with personal connections.
8. **Episode 8: "Under New Management"** – November 3, 2024
   Leadership changes bring shifts in power and loyalty within Dwight's organization.
9. **Episode 9: "Triad"** – November 10, 2024
   Dwight contends with threats from Kansas City, New York, and a new rival within Tulsa's criminal landscape.

10. **Episode 10: "Reconstruction"** – November 17, 2024
    The season finale promises to reshape Dwight's operation as he faces significant challenges and prepares for the future.

The episodes of *Tulsa King* are crafted with such depth, suspense, and rich character development that they make for amazing rewatch experiences. From the intense power plays and Dwight's gripping journey in Season 1 to the escalating stakes in Season 2, each episode unfolds with thrilling confrontations, unexpected alliances, and dynamic storytelling that reveal more layers on every viewing.

The series is packed with complex relationships and sharp dialogue that keeps you hooked, even on repeat watches. Every interaction and twist brings new details to notice, making *Tulsa King* a perfect choice for viewers who love to analyze and dive deeper into the intricate web of loyalty, power, and ambition.

<u>Message from the Author:</u>

I hope you enjoyed this book, I love astrology and knew there was not a book such as this out on the shelf. I love metaphysical items as well. Please check out my other books:

-Life of Government Benefits

-My life of Hell

-My life with Hydrocephalus

-Red Sky

-World Domination:Woman's rule

-World Domination:Woman's Rule 2: The War

-Life and Banishment of Apophis: book 1

-The Kidney Friendly Diet

-The Ultimate Hemp Cookbook

-Creating a Dispensary(legally)

-Cleanliness throughout life: the importance of showering from childhood to adulthood.

-Strong Roots: The Risks of Overcoddling children

-Hemp Horoscopes: Cosmic Insights and Earthly Healing

- Celestial Hemp Navigating the Zodiac: Through the Green Cosmos

-Astrological Hemp: Aligning The Stars with Earth's Ancient Herb

-The Astrological Guide to Hemp: Stars, Signs, and Sacred Leaves

-Green Growth: Innovative Marketing Strategies for your Hemp Products and Dispensary

-Cosmic Cannabis

-Astrological Munchies

-Henry The Hemp

-Zodiacal Roots: The Astrological Soul Of Hemp

- Green Constellations: Intersection of Hemp and Zodiac

-Hemp in The Houses: An astrological Adventure Through The Cannabis Galaxy

-Galactic Ganja Guide

Heavenly Hemp

Zodiac Leaves

Doctor Who Astrology

Cannastrology

Stellar Satvias and Cosmic Indicas

Celestial Cannabis: A Zodiac Journey

AstroHerbology: The Sky and The Soil: Volume 1

AstroHerbology:Celestial Cannabis:Volume 2

Cosmic Cannabis Cultivation

The Starry Guide to Herbal Harmony: Volume 1

The Starry Guide to Herbal Harmony: Cannabis Universe: Volume 2

Yugioh Astrology: Astrological Guide to Deck, Duels and more

Nightmare Mansion: Echoes of The Abyss

Nightmare Mansion 2: Legacy of Shadows

Nightmare Mansion 3: Shadows of the Forgotten

Nightmare Mansion 4: Echoes of the Damned

The Life and Banishment of Apophis: Book 2

Nightmare Mansion: Halls of Despair

Healing with Herb: Cannabis and Hydrocephalus

Planetary Pot: Aligning with Astrological Herbs: Volume 1

Fast Track to Freedom: 30 Days to Financial Independence Using AI, Assets, and Agile Hustles

Cosmic Hemp Pathways

How to Become Financially Free in 30 Days: 10,000 Paths to Prosperity

Zodiacal Herbage: Astrological Insights: Volume 1

Nightmare Mansion: Whispers in the Walls

The Daleks Invade Atlantis

Henry the hemp and Hydrocephalus

10X The Kidney Friendly Diet

Cannabis Universe: Adult coloring book

Hemp Astrology: The Healing Power of the Stars

Zodiacal Herbage: Astrological Insights: Cannabis Universe: Volume 2

Planetary Pot: Aligning with Astrological Herbs: Cannabis Universes: Volume 2

Doctor Who Meets the Replicators and SG-1: The Ultimate Battle for Survival

Nightmare Mansion: Curse of the Blood Moon

The Celestial Stoner: A Guide to the Zodiac

Cosmic Pleasures: Sex Toy Astrology for Every Sign

Hydrocephalus Astrology: Navigating the Stars and Healing Waters

Lapis and the Mischievous Chocolate Bar

Celestial Positions: Sexual Astrology for Every Sign

Apophis's Shadow Work Journal: : A Journey of Self-Discovery and Healing

Kinky Cosmos: Sexual Kink Astrology for Every Sign

Digital Cosmos: The Astrological Digimon Compendium

Stellar Seeds: The Cosmic Guide to Growing with Astrology

Apophis's Daily Gratitude Journal

Cat Astrology: Feline Mysteries of the Cosmos

The Cosmic Kama Sutra: An Astrological Guide to Sexual Positions

Unleash Your Potential: A Guided Journal Powered by AI Insights

Whispers of the Enchanted Grove

Cosmic Pleasures: An Astrological Guide to Sexual Kinks

369, 12 Manifestation Journal

Whisper of the nocturne journal(blank journal for writing or drawing)

The Boogey Book

Locked In Reflection: A Chastity Journey Through Locktober

Generating Wealth Quickly:

How to Generate $100,000 in 24 Hours

Star Magic: Harness the Power of the Universe

The Flatulence Chronicles: A Fart Journal for Self-Discovery

The Doctor and The Death Moth

Seize the Day: A Personal Seizure Tracking Journal

The Ultimate Boogeyman Safari: A Journey into the Boogie World and Beyond

Whispers of Samhain: 1,000 Spells of Love, Luck, and Lunar Magic: Samhain Spell Book

Apophis's guides:

Witch's Spellbook Crafting Guide for Halloween

<u>Frost & Flame: The Enchanted Yule Grimoire of 1000 Winter Spells</u>

<u>The Ultimate Boogey Goo Guide & Spooky Activities for Halloween Fun</u>

Harmony of the Scales: A Libra's Spellcraft for Balance and Beauty

The Enchanted Advent: 36 Days of Christmas Wonders

Nightmare Mansion: The Labyrinth of Screams

Harvest of Enchantment: 1,000 Spells of Gratitude, Love, and Fortune for Thanksgiving

The Boogey Chronicles: A Journal of Nightly Encounters and Shadowy Secrets

The 12 Days of Financial Freedom: A Step-by-Step Christmas Countdown to Transform Your Finances

Sigil of the Eternal Spiral Blank Journal

A Christmas Feast: Timeless Recipes for Every Meal

Holiday Stress-Free Solutions: A Survival Guide to Thriving During the Festive Season

Yu-Gi-Oh! Holiday Gifting Mastery: The Ultimate Guide for Fans and Newcomers Alike

Holiday Harmony: A Hydrocephalus Survival Guide for the Festive Season

Celestial Craft: The Witch's Almanac for 2025 – A Cosmic Guide to Manifestations, Moons, and Mystical Events

Doctor Who: The Toymaker's Winter Wonderland

If you want solar for your home go here: https://www.harborsolar.live/apophisenterprises/

Get Some Tarot cards: https://www.makeplayingcards.com/sell/apophis-occult-shop

<u>Get some shirts: https://www.bonfire.com/store/apophis-shirt-emporium/</u>

<u>Instagrams:</u>
@apophis_enterprises,
@apophisbookemporium,
@apophisscardshop
Twitter: @apophisenterpr1 Tiktok:@apophisenterprise
Youtube: @sg1fan23477, @FiresideRetreatKingdom
Hive: @sg1fan23477

Podcast: Apophis Chat Zone: https://open.spotify.com/show/
5zXbrCLEV2xzCp8ybrfHsk?si=fb4d4fdbdce44dec

Newsletter: https://apophiss-newsletter-27c897.beehiiv.com/

Get printable holiday budget planners: apophisenterprises-llc.org/Apophis-emporium-shop /ols/products/holiday-budgeting-packageprintable